Structured Derivations

Teaching Mathematical Reasoning in High School

Ralph-Johan Back

Four Ferries Publishing

Contact information

Ralph-Johan Back, Professor of Computer Science,
Abo Akademi University
Joukohaisenkatu 3 – 5, 50250 Turku, Finland
mail: backrj@abo.fi, web: www.abo.fi/~backrj

© Ralph-Johan Back, 2015. All rights reserved.

Four Ferries Publishing

ISBN 978-952-7147-00-9

Cover picture: "Tuncay". https://flic.kr/p/njc9ph.

Contents

Contents		**iii**
1	**Introduction**	**1**
2	**Basic Calculations**	**5**
	2.1 Syntax of a Calculation	11
	2.2 Expressions and Relations	13
	2.3 Justifying the Steps	14
	2.4 The Level of Detail	16
	2.5 Mathematical facts and justifications	17
	2.6 Correctness of a Calculation	19
	2.7 Assignments	21
3	**Basic Tasks**	**23**
	3.1 Questions and Answers	28
	3.2 Proof Tasks	30
	3.3 Calculation Tasks	32
	3.4 Is the Answer Correct	33
	3.5 A More Verbal Format	35
	3.6 Assignments	36
4	**General Tasks**	**39**
	4.1 Facts	39
	4.2 Definitions	43
	4.3 Correctness of Observations	45
	4.4 Solving Problems as Tasks	46
	4.5 Nested Tasks	49
	4.6 Inheritance	53
	4.7 General Syntax for Tasks	54
	4.8 Assignments	56

5 Problem Solving Paradigms — 57
- 5.1 Calculations — 57
- 5.2 Forward Derivations — 58
- 5.3 Backward Derivations — 60
- 5.4 Combining Paradigms — 61
- 5.5 Examples — 63
- 5.6 Assignments — 69

6 Word Problems — 71
- 6.1 Word Problems as Tasks — 71
- 6.2 Is the Solution Correct — 77
- 6.3 Assignments — 78

7 Structured Derivations — 81
- 7.1 Generalizing Tasks to Structured Derivations — 82
- 7.2 Modeling with Structured Derivations — 85
- 7.3 Example from Geometry — 88
- 7.4 Example from Probability Theory — 91
- 7.5 Example from Mechanics — 93
- 7.6 Example from Nuclear Physics — 95
- 7.7 Assignments — 98

8 Checking Correctness — 101
- 8.1 Correctness of Tasks — 101
- 8.2 Correctness of Structured Derivations — 105
- 8.3 Checklists for Structured Derivations — 107

9 Background on Structured Derivations — 111

A Syntax — 115
- A.1 Derivations — 115
- A.2 Assumptions — 116
- A.3 Observations — 116
- A.4 Tasks — 117
- A.5 Calculations — 119
- A.6 Justifications — 120
- A.7 What Has Not Been Defined — 120
- A.8 Abstract Syntax of Structured Derivations — 121

B Answers to assignments — 123

Bibliography — 127

Acknowledgements

My research on structured derivations started as part of a long and fruitful cooperation with Joakim von Wright, when we were working on a monograph on refinement calculus in the 1990s. Much of the later research on structured derivations was carried out in the *Learning and Reasoning Laboratory,* a joint research laboratory at the IT-departments of Åbo Akademi University and University of Turku.

Most of the ideas presented in this book have taken form during long and detailed discussions with a large number of people. In particular, I want to thank Stefan Asikainen, Linda Mannila, Mia Peltomäki, Viorel Preoteasa, Tapio Salakoski, Petri Sallasmaa, Petri Salmela, Patrik Sibelius and Joakim von Wright for the many insightful and critical discussions we have had during the years, about mathematics education in general and about structured derivations in particular, for all the improvements they have suggested and for their criticism of properties that can be improved. I want to thank Stefan Asikainen for providing the assignments for the book, Joonatan Jalonen, Marie Linden-Slotte, and Anton Tarasyuk for careful reading and commenting on the preliminary drafts of the book and Jenna Lainio for helping with the layoout. The development of e-books and software for structured derivations has been done as teamwork, with a highly dedicated and skilled research team. I wish to thank everyone who have been working in this team, which, in addition to the ones already mentioned above, also includes Johannes Eriksson, Kim Gustafsson, Kadri Hiob, Terhi Hovi, Topi Hurtig, Matti Hutri, Esbjörn Hägerstedt, Tero Kesäläinen, Siiri Künnapas, Antti Lempinen, Rolf Linden, Saara Mäkinen, Mari Pöld, Teemu Rajala, Tom Rydell, Eva Rönnqvist, Ida Schauman, Josefin Vidjeskog, Solveig Wallin, and Lars Wingård.

I also want to thank the numerous high school teachers and students in Finland, Sweden and Estonia who have participated in our pilot studies on mathematics courses based on structured derivations. They have given us plenty of valuable feedback, that has inspired and motivated further development of the method.

The research on structured derivations has been financed by the Academy of Finland, TEKES (the Finnish Funding Agency for Technology and Innovation), the Technology Industries of Finland Centennial Foundation, the Finnish National Board of Education, the EU Central Baltic Program and the Swedish Cultural Foundation in Finland. I want to extend my gratitude to each of these organizations, who with their support have helped to advance the method from theoretical ideas on how to structure mathematical arguments to comprehensive mathematics course books based on structured derivations, the development of an interactive e-book environment to support these course books, numerous teachers training courses on structured derivations, and extensive piloting of the ideas expressed here in practical mathematics courses at different education levels.

Last but not least, I want to thank my wife, Barbro Back, for many many discussions and her unwavering support throughout the research on and development of structured derivations.

CHAPTER 1

Introduction

Mathematics is based on proofs. The proof shows the logical reasoning behind a theorem, allows us to understand the meaning of it, its limitations and its consequences. Without a proof, a theorem is like magic; with a proof it is (sometimes more, sometimes less) self evident. But proofs are considered difficult in mathematics education of today, in particular at secondary level, and are therefore often avoided in teaching. When proofs are given, they are often informal and the underlying logic is not explicated.

The purpose of this book is to put forward an alternative method for teaching mathematics at secondary and tertiary level that reintroduces proofs and careful argumentation as the solid basis for mathematics education. The method, *structured derivations*, is essentially a format for presenting mathematical arguments (calculations, derivations, proofs, etc). The format is designed to show the overall structure of the argument, while at the same time allowing a detailed inspection of each step in the argument. The method does not put any restrictions on the mathematical domain where the argumentation is carried out, nor on the level of detail or mathematical rigor of the argumentation. Hence, structured derivations can be used in any area of mathematics, and at any level of education.

Structured derivations are based on a precise format for writing proofs and derivations. The method is a further development of the *calculational proof style* originally proposed by Edsger W. Dijkstra and his colleagues Wim Feijen, Netty van Gasteren, and Carel Scholten [11, 28] (see [12] for a nice overview of the calculational proof style). They present a proof in a fixed format, as a sequence of calculation steps, with an explicit justification for each step. The original motivation for this proof style was to provide a simpler and more intuitive way of reasoning about program correctness [8, 4].

Structured derivations extend the calculational proof style by combining the three main proof paradigms, *forward proofs*, *backward proofs* and *calculations*, into a single unified proof method [3]. Structured derivations were also originally developed for proofs about program correctness, in this case in the refinement calculus [1, 8, 2]. Later, this proof style was found to be quite useful also for teaching mathematics i general, in particular at the secondary and tertiary education level [9, 5, 24].

1. Introduction

The design of structured derivations has been gradually modified by our experiences of teaching mathematics with this approach. The aim has been to make the syntax as intuitive and transparent as possible for students. The language of structured derivations presented in this book is a considerable development and extension of the original approach, and provides a standard format for many different kinds of mathematical arguments, from numerical calculations and algebraic derivations to mathematical proofs and general problem solving.

The primary application for structured derivations is for teaching mathematics, from junior high school to freshman courses at the university. We have tried to make the derivation style easy to read, easy to understand, easy to write and easy to check for errors. Structured derivations can be introduced in class education without much explanations, as the way the teacher prefers to write down and structure his/her own argumentation. The most important contribution of structured derivations (already present in the calculational proof style) is that each derivation step is explicitly justified. This makes it easier to follow and understand the argumentation, compared to the standard way where only selected steps are explicitly justified. Explicit justifications make it easier for students to understand a derivation afterwards, when working on assignments or preparing for an exam, and to check and find errors in their own derivations. Structured derivations provide a standardized format for presenting mathematical argumentation, so that students can concentrate on solving the problem at hand, and not on invent a presentation format for the solution on the fly.

Structured derivations are intended to be used for all kinds of mathematics courses, and at different level of mathematical rigor. A structured derivation provides a specific format (syntax) for how to present a mathematical argument, and an exact meaning (semantics) to any proof constructed in this format. But it does not fix the underlying mathematical domain. A derivation uses the standard notation and definitions of the underlying domain, together with the available theorems. The level of rigor at which the argumentation is carried out can be chosen freely, varying from informal argumentation to precise and exact mathematical proofs. At one extreme, we can easily write standard informal mathematical arguments as structured derivations. At the other extreme, we can use structured derivations to express completely axiomatic, machine checkable proofs.

Structured derivations have been designed with computer support in mind. The syntax is defined precisely, so that it can be parsed by a computer. This makes it possible to check that a proof is syntactically correct. We can also mechanically translate a structured derivation into a standard natural deduction proof. This means that it is possible to use computers to automatically check the correctness of a structured derivation, provided the underlying mathematics of the derivation has been mechanized, i.e., formalized in a way that that can be used by automatic theorem provers. Large areas of mathematics have in fact already been mechanized and are checkable by automated theorem provers like HOL, Isabelle, PVS, Coq, or Z3.

Structured derivations are intended to support all kinds of mathematical arguments, like proofs, calculations, derivations, geometric construction, and so on. The scale is from small simple exercises to large and complex proofs. The format is based on a hierarchical view of a derivation, where the main derivation can be split up into a number of more detailed observations and derivations nested inside the main derivation, which in turn can be further split up into even more detailed observations and nested derivations, and so on. The ideal tool for working with structured derivations is an outlining editor, where the user can selectively show and hide observations and sub-derivations at different levels of detail.

The structured derivations method has been developed in a tight feedback loop with empirical studies. These studies have been mostly carried out at high school level, but we have also done pilots at junior high school and at university level. This work started already in 2001, with teaching a number of mathematics courses in high school using structured derivations. The results of these pilot courses were generally very positive and encouraging. The structured derivation method has been taught in a large number of teachers continued education courses financed by the Finnish National Board of Education. The method was further developed in a large EU project (E-math 2011 – 13), where the method was piloted in a number of high schools in Finland, Sweden and Estonia. The students learn quickly how to use the proof format in their own solutions, and they appreciate the added clarity gained, both when they use the format themselves, as well as when the teacher presents examples in this style [6, 20]. We also see definite performance improvements in their mathematics courses when the method is used [24]. Based on the encouraging results from our pilot studies, we are presently creating a completely new textbook series for high school mathematics that is based on using structured derivations throughout the curriculum. More background and references to structured derivations and their application in practice is given in the last chapter of the book.

The examples in the book are mostly taken from standard high school mathematics courses (K10 – 12), while a few are taken from earlier courses (K7 – 9). The method is presented in stages, so that Chapters 2 and 3 describe the basic approach, applicable from K7 onwards. Chapters 4 – 6 describe tools for creating and organizing more complex mathematical derivations. This material would generally be needed at high school level, from K10 onwards. Chapters 7 and 8 then discuss mathematical modeling and solving word problems in more detail, and show how to apply mathematics to general problem solving. This material is intended for high schools and beyond. The final chapter gives more information about the background of structured derivation, related work and activities, and gives pointers to further reading.

Chapter 2

Basic Calculations

Let us start by introducing *structured calculations*, a simple form of structured derivations. Consider the following basic task: calculate the value of the expression $3 \cdot 2^3 + 4 \cdot 3^2 - 2 \cdot 4^2$. A traditional solution may look like this:

$$
\begin{aligned}
& 3 \cdot 2^3 + 4 \cdot 3^2 - 2 \cdot 4^2 \\
=\ & 3 \cdot 8 + 4 \cdot 9 - 2 \cdot 16 \\
=\ & 24 + 36 - 32 \\
=\ & 60 - 32 \\
=\ & 28
\end{aligned}
$$

We rewrite this as a *structured calculation*, as follows:

- $\quad 3 \cdot 2^3 + 4 \cdot 3^2 - 2 \cdot 4^2$
- = {calculate the powers}
  $3 \cdot 8 + 4 \cdot 9 - 2 \cdot 16$
- = {carry out the multiplications}
  $24 + 36 - 32$
- = {carry out the first addition}
  $60 - 32$
- = {carry out the subtraction}
  28

□

2. Basic Calculations

The solution is the same as above, but now each step is justified explicitly. A justification is written on separate line and is enclosed in curly brackets. The justification explains why equality holds between the expressions on the previous line and the next line. The first step thus says that

$$3 \cdot 2^3 + 4 \cdot 3^2 - 2 \cdot 4^2 = 3 \cdot 8 + 4 \cdot 9 - 2 \cdot 16$$

which we get by calculating the powers.

The calculation is written in two columns: the equality sign is in the first column, while expressions and justifications are written in the second column. The two column format is used throughout in structured derivations. The *bullet* "•" indicates the start of the calculation, and the *square* "□" the end of it.

It is, of course, possible to give explicit justifications in the traditional format too:

$$
\begin{array}{rll}
 & 3 \cdot 2^3 + 4 \cdot 3^2 - 2 \cdot 4^2 & \text{calculate the powers} \\
= & 3 \cdot 8 + 4 \cdot 9 - 2 \cdot 16 & \text{perform the multiplications} \\
= & 24 + 36 - 32 & \text{perform the addition} \\
= & 60 - 32 & \text{perform the subtraction} \\
= & 28 &
\end{array}
$$

The justification is here written on the same line as the expression. The problem with this format is that it does not allow for longer expressions and/or justifications. Justifications are easy to omit, in particular for steps that seem more or less obvious, so there are usually few or no justifications in the calculation. But there is a problem with selective justifications: what is obvious to someone writing the calculation may not be obvious to the one who tries to understand it. A calculation without justifications is harder to understand. Even if you made the calculation yourself, it may still be hard to check the calculation afterwards, when you have forgotten the reasoning behind the calculation. Even an obvious explanation, such as "perform the addition" in the calculation above, can provide useful information to the inexperienced, it shows that there is no hidden complexity in this step.

The simpler format with few or no justifications rarely causes problems for an experienced mathematician, he/she will quickly see what rules were used in each step and how. But for a student who is just trying to learn something, the lack of justifications is an additional hurdle. It makes it more difficult to follow the reasoning, thus lowering the motivation for learning and decreasing the confidence in understanding the issues at hand. Problems in learning mathematics may often be due to a communication problem like this, rather than too weak motivation, inability to focus, or lack of mathematical ability.

The traditional method of teaching mathematics, used for centuries, is that the teacher writes calculations and arguments on the blackboard, and the students copy these into their notebooks. The teacher justifies each step of the calculation verbally. The students, however, only copy what the teacher writes on the blackboard, they do not write down the verbal justifications. The teacher thinks that he/she is giving the whole story, but the students only write down half of it. When students later do their homework, they start by looking at the examples that the teacher presented, trying to reconstruct the justification for each step. The best students will manage this, sharpening their understanding of mathematics in the process. But other students, who lack motivation, or have not done their previous homework properly, will run into problems. They create a backlog of unresolved issues, derivation steps not understood because of some misunderstanding or confusion about the underlying mathematics. The problems pile up as the course progresses, since there are more and more steps in the teacher's examples that the student does not understand. And these problems carry over to the next course. These students will gradually lose confidence in their ability to master mathematics, and classify themselves as bad at math. Mathematics teaching then becomes a process where we filter out the future mathematicians, those who will go on to study sciences, engineering and medicine. The rest are left on their own, they have failed at math and will in future studies avoid all subjects that even smell of mathematics.

Structured derivations try to solve this communication problem. Understanding the calculation afterwards becomes easier when we justify each step explicitly. Even students who were absent, unable, or unwilling to pay attention when the teacher showed the calculation for the first time, can now understand the calculation steps on their own. A step without justification is also easy to spot in a structured derivation, an empty line indicates that the calculation is incomplete. The format forces both students and teachers to write out the justification for each step explicitly.

There are more reasons for insisting that each step is explicitly justified. The students usually have or will get access to the correct answers to their assignments. This can give them the impression that getting the correct answer is all that matters. But calculations in real life are carried out precisely when we do not know the answer; there is no reason to calculate if we already know the answer. The only way to convince ourselves and others that we have found the correct answer is then to carefully check that each step of the calculation is correct, i.e., check that the justification for each step is correct and that we have not made any errors in calculating the next step.

The traditional calculation format (even with added justifications) requires fewer lines than a structured derivation, and it looks more concise. However, the number of symbols in the two calculations are roughly the same. So we do not save any ink or keystrokes with the traditional calculation format, only some paper.

Our example calculation above is simple and trivial, so the explicit justifications may seem unnecessary. But the calculation may not be that simple and obvious for a student who is, e.g., learning about powers for the first time. We illustrate the need for explicit justifications with another, less trivial example, where the calculation steps are not as obvious.

Example 1. We want to calculate the tangent of the expression $\frac{17\pi}{3}$. We start by

2. Basic Calculations

giving a solution in the traditional format, without explicit justifications.

$$\begin{aligned}
\tan \frac{17\pi}{3} &= \tan\left(\frac{6 \cdot 2\pi + 5\pi}{3}\right) \\
&= \tan\left(2 \cdot 2\pi + \frac{5\pi}{3}\right) \\
&= \tan \frac{5\pi}{3} \\
&= \tan\left(2\pi - \frac{\pi}{3}\right) \\
&= -\tan \frac{\pi}{3} \\
&= -\sqrt{3}
\end{aligned}$$

The same argumentation, but written as a structured derivation:

- $\tan \frac{17\pi}{3}$

$=$ {factor out 2π}

$\tan\left(\dfrac{6 \cdot 2\pi + 5\pi}{3}\right)$

$=$ {write the angle in the form $n \cdot 2\pi + \alpha$}

$\tan\left(2 \cdot 2\pi + \dfrac{5\pi}{3}\right)$

$=$ {we can ignore full circles 2π}

$\tan \dfrac{5\pi}{3}$

$=$ {the angle is in the fourth quadrant, so we can write it in the form $2\pi - \alpha_0$ where α_0 is between $0°$ and $90°$}

$\tan\left(2\pi - \dfrac{\pi}{3}\right)$

$=$ {ignore full circles, $\tan\left(-\frac{\pi}{3}\right) = -\tan\left(\frac{\pi}{3}\right)$}

$-\tan \dfrac{\pi}{3}$

$=$ {this is a 30 - 60 - 90 triangle}

$-\sqrt{3}$

□

The explicit justifications makes it easier to understand the argumentation. Writing the justification on a separate line gives us enough room to properly explain each step. The structured calculation format allows for terms and explanations that stretch over two or more lines, without compromising ease of reading. (We use a black square to the right on a page to indicate the end of an example, a definition or a theorem).

Calculations like the one above are based on the fact that equality is *transitive*. This means that for arbitrary values $a_1, a_2, \ldots, a_n$: if $a_1 = a_2$, $a_2 = a_3$, $\ldots$, and $a_{n-1} = a_n$, then $a_1 = a_n$.

We will give a few more examples of calculations at high school level. Analysis is an area where calculations prove to be very efficient for solving problems.

Example 2. Calculate
$$\lim_{x \to 1} \frac{x-1}{\sqrt{x^2+3}-2}$$

We notice that the denominator is 0, when $x = 1$, so we have to manipulate the expression into a form where this does not happen.

- $\lim_{x \to 1} \frac{x-1}{\sqrt{x^2+3}-2}$

= {eliminate the radical from the denominator by expanding with $\sqrt{x^2+3}+2$}

$\lim_{x \to 1} \frac{(x-1)(\sqrt{x^2+3}+2)}{(\sqrt{x^2+3}+2)(\sqrt{x^2+3}-2)}$

= {use the rule $(a-b)(a+b) = a^2 - b^2$}

$\lim_{x \to 1} \frac{(x-1)(\sqrt{x^2+3}+2)}{(\sqrt{x^2+3})^2 - 2^2}$

= {simplify the denominator}

$\lim_{x \to 1} \frac{(x-1)(\sqrt{x^2+3}+2)}{x^2-1}$

= {write the denominator in the form $(x-1)(x+1)$}

$\lim_{x \to 1} \frac{(x-1)(\sqrt{x^2+3}+2)}{(x-1)(x+1)}$

= {we can cancel out $(x-1)$}

$\lim_{x \to 1} \frac{\sqrt{x^2+3}+2}{x+1}$

= {calculate the limit by substituting $x = 1$}

$\frac{\sqrt{1^2+3}+2}{1+1}$

= {calculate the value}

2

■

2. Basic Calculations

The answer follows again from the transitivity of equality:

$$\lim_{x \to 1} \frac{x-1}{\sqrt{x^2+3}-2} = 2$$

∎

Solving an equation is another example where we typically use calculations. The purpose of an arithmetic calculation is to determine the value of an arithmetic expression, or to transform it into a simpler expression that has the same value as the original one. Equations are not arithmetic but logical statements, i.e., statements that are either true or false, depending on the values of the unknown variables. The equation $x + 2 = 2x - 1$ is, e.g., true for some values of x (the roots of the equation) and false for all other values.

Solving an equation means that we simplify the equation into a form where we can directly see which variable values satisfy the equation. The solution and the original equation should be *equivalent* to each other, i.e., be equally true for every value of x. Then the two equations have the same roots. We denote equivalence by "$\equiv$" (double implication "$\Leftrightarrow$" is maybe more common, but we prefer "$\equiv$" because it more clearly shows that this is an equality between truth values).

Example 3. Solve the equation $x + 2 = 2x - 1$.

We solve the equation by transforming it step by step into an equivalent form where the solution is explicitly shown. Note that we use "$\equiv$" for equivalence between logical statements, rather than the more common "$\Leftrightarrow$". The reason is that equivalence really is just equality between the truth values of logical statements. We want to emphasize this by using a notation that is as close as possible to the traditional sign for equality.

- $\qquad x + 2 = 2x - 1$
- $\equiv \qquad \{\text{add } -2 \text{ to both sides of the equation}\}$
- $\qquad x + 2 - 2 = 2x - 1 - 2$
- $\equiv \qquad \{\text{simplify both sides}\}$
- $\qquad x = 2x - 3$
- $\equiv \qquad \{\text{add } -2x \text{ to both sides of the equation}\}$
- $\qquad x - 2x = 2x - 3 - 2x$
- $\equiv \qquad \{\text{simplify both sides}\}$
- $\qquad -x = -3$
- $\equiv \qquad \{\text{divide both sides by } -1\}$
- $\qquad \dfrac{-x}{-1} = \dfrac{-3}{-1}$

$\equiv$ {simplify}

$x = 3$

□

Adding the same expression to both sides of an equation does not change the truth value of the equation, regardless of the value of x. Similarly, the truth value of the equation is preserved when we multiply both sides by the same expression (provided it is not 0). Finally, the truth value of the equation is also preserved when we replace an arithmetic expression in an equation by another expression with the same value. Since equivalence is also transitive, the calculation shows that

$$(x + 2 = 2x - 1) \equiv (x = 3)$$

In other words, $x = 3$ is the solution to the equation. ∎

We can also use a calculation to prove a theorem. For instance, the next calculation proves the conjugate rule for binomials.

Example 4. Show that $(a + b)(a - b) = a^2 - b^2$. We show this with the following calculation:

- $(a + b)(a - b)$
- = {the distributive law for polynomials}

  $(a + b)a - (a + b)b$
- = {the distributive law for polynomials}

  $a^2 + ba - ab - b^2$
- = {the second and third terms cancel out}

  $a^2 - b^2$

□

The transitivity of equality then shows that the theorem is true. ∎

2.1 Syntax of a Calculation

A *structured calculation* is written in a specific way. The calculation is written in two columns. The bullet starts the calculation, and the square shows where it ends. The initial mathematical expression is written in the second column. On the next line we write a relation in the first column (denoted *rel*, this can, e.g., be "=" or "≤" or "≡") followed by a justification in the second column. A new mathematical expression is then written on the next line, in the second column. We continue in this way, until we have reached the final mathematical expression. The syntax of a structured calculation is thus as follows:

2. BASIC CALCULATIONS

    calculation
-    *expression*
rel   *justification*
    expression
⋮
rel   *justification*
    expression
□

We have used color coding for the different syntactic categories in the calculation: red for relations, blue for justifications, and black for expressions. The three vertical dots show that we can add 0 or more steps to the first calculation step. Every subsequent calculation step has two lines, a relation and justification line followed by an expression line. The justification explains why the relation shown in the first column holds between the expression on the preceding line and the expression on the next line. The justifications in our examples so far have been simple, just explaining text enclosed in curly brackets. We will later encounter more complex justifications. Below is an example of a structured derivation with 4 steps.

•	*expression*	•	$3 \cdot 2^3 + 4 \cdot 3^2 - 2 \cdot 4^2$
rel	*justification*	=	{calculate the powers}
	expression		$3 \cdot 8 + 4 \cdot 9 - 2 \cdot 16$
rel	*justification*	=	{perform the multiplications}
	expression		$24 + 36 - 32$
rel	*justification*	=	{perform the addition}
	expression		$60 - 32$
rel	*justification*	=	{perform the subtraction}
	expression		28
□		□	

On the left we show the general format, and on the right an example of a structured calculation that follow this syntax.

The calculation to the right says that

$$3 \cdot 2^3 + 4 \cdot 3^2 - 2 \cdot 4^2 \;=\; 3 \cdot 8 + 4 \cdot 9 - 2 \cdot 16$$
$$\text{and}$$
$$3 \cdot 8 + 4 \cdot 9 - 2 \cdot 16 \;=\; 24 + 36 - 32$$
$$\text{and}$$
$$24 + 36 - 32 \;=\; 60 - 32$$
$$\text{and}$$
$$60 - 32 \;=\; 28$$

From this we can then conclude that

$$3 \cdot 2^3 + 4 \cdot 3^2 - 2 \cdot 4^2 = 28$$

since equality is transitive.

2.2 Expressions and Relations

Calculations are performed within the framework of some branch of mathematics, like algebra, geometry, analytic geometry, etc. The underlying theory will then determines the notation we use, i.e., what kind of expressions and relations we can use in the calculation. For polynomials, we use expressions like $x^2 + 2x - y + 1$ and $\dfrac{x^2 - y}{x + 2y}$, in analytic geometry we have expressions that describe lines (e.g., equations) and points (coordinates), etc. In addition to standard mathematical expressions, we can also use informal expressions like "the circumference of the circle $+ \; 3$" or "the base $\cdot$ the height of the triangle", to make the solutions more intuitive. An example of this is the following start of a derivation:

$$\quad \text{area of the triangle}$$
$$= \quad \{\text{area formula}\}$$
$$\quad \dfrac{\text{base} \,\cdot\, \text{height of the triangle}}{2}$$
$$= \quad \{\text{the height of the triangle is 3 times longer than the base according to the assumption}\}$$
$$\quad \dfrac{3 \cdot (\text{base of the triangle })^2}{2}$$
$$\vdots$$

We are free to use any binary relations between the terms. Typically, we use transitive order relations like $\leq, <, \geq, \ldots$, equality $=$, and logical relations like implication

2. BASIC CALCULATIONS

($\Rightarrow$) or equivalence ($\equiv$ or $\Leftrightarrow$). We are free to mix different binary relations in the same derivation.

Equality can be combined with any binary relation: if the relation $a \sim b$ holds and $b = c$, then $a \sim c$ also holds. Consider, e.g., the chain

$$a = b < c < d = e = f$$

This says that

$$a = b \text{ and } b < c \text{ and } c < d \text{ and } d = e \text{ and } e = f$$

We conclude that $a < f$, since $<$ is transitive.

We can also use non-transitive relations between the terms. For instance, assume that $a \to_k b$ says that the distance from a to b is k kilometers. The calculation

$$a \to_{12} b \to_8 c \to_7 d$$

then says that

$$a \to_{12} b \text{ and } b \to_8 c \text{ and } c \to_7 d$$

We conclude that the distance from a to d is $12 + 8 + 7 = 27$ km, if we drive through b and c, i.e.,

$$a \to_{27} d$$

This is an example of a conclusion we can draw from a calculation that is not based on transitivity.

Inequality is an example of a relation that is not transitive: $a \neq b$ and $b \neq c$ does not imply that $a \neq c$ (counterexample: $0 \neq 1$ and $1 \neq 0$ do not imply that $0 \neq 0$). This restricts the usefulness of multiple inequalities in structured derivations. Similarly, mixing "$\leq$" and "$\geq$" in the same derivation is usually not a good idea: from

$$a \leq b \geq c$$

we can only conclude that $a \leq b$ and $c \leq b$, i.e., that b is the largest of the numbers a, b, c.

2.3 Justifying the Steps

There are basically two different ways of justifying a calculation step. Let us assume that we have a calculation that is carried out in a context that includes the algebraic laws for addition and multiplication. We can justify a calculation step with a mathematical rule, or we can refer to a permissible operation. In the first case, the justification states which rule is used:

$$\begin{aligned} & (x+1)(x+y) \\ = \ & \{\text{the distributive law for polynomials}\} \\ & (x+1)x + (x+1)y \end{aligned}$$

2.3. Justifying the Steps

In the second case, the justification states the operation that we apply:

$$(x+1)(x+y)$$
$$= \{\text{distribute the first term across the second term}\}$$
$$(x+1)x + (x+1)y$$

In the second case, we know that distributing the first term across the second term is permissible, since the distributive law holds. An operation is allowed if there is a rule that says that the operation results in a new term that has the desired relation to the original term. In our example, we start from the term $(x+1)(x+y)$ and distribute the first term $(x+1)$ across the second term $(x+y)$. The result is a new expression $(x+1)x + (x+1)y$. The operation is permitted, since distribution preserves equality between terms, i.e.,

$$(x+1)(x+y) = (x+1)x + (x+1)y$$

holds according to the distributive law.

Both ways of explaining a step are useful but they have different characteristics. In the first case, we see the justification as a static observation of why the equality holds. In the second case, we justify why transforming an expression in a specific way is permissible. When the relation is equality, we are allowed to transform the original expression as long as we do not change the value of the expression.

The level of detail in a justification depends on whom we are trying to convince. If the reader is an experienced mathematician, a short and concise explanation may be enough, as in the examples above. If the purpose of the derivation is to illustrate how we use a certain rule, we can be more careful, e.g., by explicitly stating the rule in the justification:

$$(x+1)(x+y)$$
$$= \{\text{the distributive law for polynomials: } a(b+c) = ab + ac\}$$
$$(x+1)x + (x+1)y$$

If we want to be even more explicit, we can also say how the rule is applied:

$$(x+1)(x+y)$$
$$= \{\text{the distributive law for polynomials: } a(b+c) = ab + ac, \text{ where } a \text{ is } x+1, b \text{ is } x \text{ and } c \text{ is } y\}$$
$$(x+1)x + (x+1)y$$

Mathematical rules are often conditional. For instance, the rule for expanding and reducing fractions state that

$$\frac{a}{b} = \frac{k \cdot a}{k \cdot b}, \text{ when } k \neq 0$$

2. BASIC CALCULATIONS

When a conditional rule is used, the justification has to explain why the condition is satisfied, e.g., like this:

$$\frac{x^2+3}{x-2}$$
$$= \quad \{\text{expand the fraction by } x-1, \text{ permitted since } x > 1 \text{ by assumption, so } x-1 \neq 0\}$$
$$\frac{(x-1)(x^2+3)}{(x-1)(x-2)}$$

The justification refers to an assumption (stated elsewhere) that implies that the expansion is permitted.

The justifications that we use here, textual explanations in curly brackets, are quite simple. We will later encounter more complex justifications, where the simple explanation is expanded into a full-blown proof that the calculation step is correct. But for the moment, this simple notion of a justification is quite adequate.

2.4 The Level of Detail

The level of detail in a calculation may vary, depending on the target audience. A teacher can do the parts of the calculation that illustrate new concepts in small and detailed steps, while the parts that are based on earlier material can be done in larger steps. The calculation should, however, always be detailed enough so that an interested reader can directly check every step of the proof without having to do complicated calculations in head or on paper. This makes it easier to follow the calculation and also prevents a lot of trivial mistakes when constructing the calculation.

Example 5. We want to calculate the value of $2^8 + 2^7$. The following calculation shows the main steps, with explanations. The target audience would be students in secondary schools:

- $\quad 2^8 + 2^7$
- $=\quad$ {the product rule: $a^m a^n = a^{m+n}$, and $2^1 = 2$}
- $\quad 2 \cdot 2^7 + 2^7$
- $=\quad$ {factor out 2^7}
- $\quad (2+1) \cdot 2^7$
- $=\quad$ {calculate the value, $2^7 = 128$}
- $\quad 384$

□

Example 6. A more detailed calculation may look like this:

-     $2^8 + 2^7$
- =   {the product rule: $a^m a^n = a^{m+n}$}

      $2^1 \cdot 2^7 + 2^7$
- =   {$a = 1 \cdot a$}

      $2^1 \cdot 2^7 + 1 \cdot 2^7$
- =   {the distributive law: $(a+b)c = ac + bc$}

      $(2^1 + 1) \cdot 2^7$
- =   {power rule: $a^1 = a$}

      $(2 + 1) \cdot 2^7$
- =   {arithmetics: $1 + 2 = 3$}

      $3 \cdot 2^7$
- =   {arithmetics: $2^7 = 128$}

      $3 \cdot 128$
- =   {arithmetics: $3 \cdot 128 = 384$}

      384

□

Here every step is justified by an explicit rule. This is a suitable level of detail when the purpose is to illustrate the rules for manipulating arithmetic expressions in a more axiomatic context. The earlier level of detail was sufficient if the purpose was just to calculate the value of the expression. ∎

2.5 Mathematical facts and justifications

The calculations above are correct, if each calculation step is correct. But how do we check that a calculation step is correct. Each calculation step should be based on some mathematical fact or rule that is considered (by the author and the reader) to be obviously true. A mathematical fact is again based on some context of known mathematical properties. Typical contexts could, e.g., be arithmetic, Euclidean geometry, trigonometry, calculus, group theory, probability theory, etc. We may consider a context as just a list of mathematical definitions and laws. The justification of a step is then based on this context. A justification could be just a reference to some mathematical fact (law, theorem, definition) in the context, or it could be a complex proof of the property, in this context.

2. Basic Calculations

Let us introduce a notation for this. We write

$$\Phi \vdash Q \text{ by } J$$

to express that *justification J proves* the *property Q* in the *context* Φ. More precisely, J is a proof of the fact that Q is true when all properties in Φ are true. Alternatively, we can say that Q *follows from* Φ by J, or that Φ *implies* Q because of J.

Ultimately, any mathematical argument is broken down to a collection of basic mathematical facts that we accept as true. We can see these basic facts as the Lego bricks of mathematics. More complex mathematical arguments are constructed by putting these basic bricks together, following specific construction rules that guarantee that the result is also a mathematical fact.

For us, a *basic mathematical fact* is of the form

$$\Phi \vdash Q \text{ by } \{explanation\}$$

where *explanation* is a piece of text that explains why Q must be true in the context Φ.[1] This fact is accepted as it is, it is not broken down into more basic facts.

We consider a context as just a sequence of assumptions, facts and definitions and use Φ as the general symbol for contexts. We can extend a given context Φ with another list Φ' of assumptions, facts and definitions. The combined list is then denoted Φ, Φ'. We will discuss contexts, how they are used and how they are constructed in more detail in Chapter 7.

Example 7. (a) Let Φ_1 stand for the the definitions and theorems of trigonometry, together with basic arithmetic properties. A basic mathematical fact could then be, e.g.,

$$\Phi_1 \vdash \tan \frac{17\pi}{3} = \tan\left(\frac{6 \cdot 2\pi + 5\pi}{3}\right) \text{ \{factor out } 2\pi\}$$

(b) Let Φ_2 stand for the basic algebraic properties of operations on real numbers. The following is an example of a basic mathematical fact:

$$\Phi_2 \vdash (a+b)(a-b) = (a+b)a - (a+b)b \text{ \{the distributive law for polynomials\}}$$

(c) Let Φ_2 again stands for the basic algebraic properties of real numbers. Then the following would be an example of a basic mathematical fact:

---

[1] The notation says that property Q is provably true in the context Φ, and that the proof is given by *explanation*. We could also write $\Phi \vdash Q$ {*explanation*} as

$$\vdash \wedge \Phi \Rightarrow Q \text{ \{}explanation\}$$

i.e., that the conjunction of all assumptions in Φ implies Q, because of *explanation*. The $\vdash$ symbol is used in logic to express that a proposition is provable. Here we say that *explanation* is the proof.

$$\Phi_2, x > 1 \vdash \frac{x^2+3}{x-2} = \frac{(x-1)(x^2+3)}{(x-1)(x-2)} \quad \{\text{expand the fraction by } x-1\}$$

Note that the context also includes the assumption $x > 1$. This guarantees that $x - 1 \neq 0$, so that the fraction remains well-defined after expansion. ■

As we illustrated in Section 2.4, the level of detail may vary in mathematical proofs. This means that what is considered a basic mathematical fact varies from one person to another. What a trained mathematician regards as a basic mathematical fact may well require a more detailed argument for somebody who is just learning the mathematical topic at hand.

Ultimately, there must be some basic mathematical facts that we all accept as true, without further proofs. These facts belong to the realm of *Logic*, the theory of rational (or common sense) reasoning. There we list a number of basic facts that we accept as true without further justification, and present the rules by which these basic facts can be combined into more complex arguments. The sequel to this book is devoted to showing that structured derivations together with a modicum of logic forms a very practical and useful tool for doing mathematics, applicable already at high school level. There we also give an exact definition of what it means for Q to follow from Φ by *justification*, in a logical setting.

We want to avoid going too deeply into logic in this book, so we will take $\Phi \vdash Q \{explanation\}$ as a primitive notion. We interpret it as a statement of a basic mathematical fact, a fact that the person constructing the proof takes for granted and that the reader of the derivation is assumed to accept as true. We see *structured derivations* as providing us with the architectural principles for building more complex mathematical facts from such basic mathematical facts. Whether a mathematical fact constructed with as a structured derivation is correct or not depends ultimately on whether each basic mathematical fact used in the derivation is correct or not. If each basic fact is correct, then the structured derivation as a whole will also be correct, and proves the mathematical fact in question.

2.6 Correctness of a Calculation

When is a calculation correct? We first define what it means for a calculation step to be correct.

Definition 1. A *calculation step*

$$\begin{array}{rl} & t \\ \sim & \{justification\} \\ & t' \end{array}$$

is *correct* in *context* Φ, if $\Phi \vdash t \sim t'$ by *justification*. In other words, the calculation step is correct if *justification* proves that $t \sim t'$ in the context Φ.

A *calculation* is then *correct* in a *context* Φ, if each calculation step is correct in this context. ■

2. BASIC CALCULATIONS

A general calculation is of the form

$$
\begin{array}{rl}
\bullet & t_0 \\
\sim_1 & \textit{justification}_1 \\
& t_1 \\
\sim_2 & \textit{justification}_2 \\
& t_2 \\
& \vdots \\
& t_{n-1} \\
\sim_n & \textit{justification}_n \\
& t_n \\
\square &
\end{array}
$$

where $t_0, t_1, \ldots, t_n$ are mathematical expressions, and $\sim_1, \ldots, \sim_n$ are binary relations, $n \geq 1$. We assume that the calculation is carried out in some specific *context* Φ.

This calculation is just a sequence of calculation steps. The conclusion that we draw from these calculation steps is not part of the calculation (we will introduce a place for the conclusions later on). This means that we may have different binary relations in each step. The advantage of having the same transitive relation $\sim$ (or equality) in each step is that it we may then conclude that $t_0 \sim t_n$. This is by far the most common use in structured calculations. Equality (when we calculate the value of an expression or simplify it) and equivalence (when we solve equations) are also the most common relations in calculations.

Our definition of correctness means that a calculation step is considered wrong even if the mathematical fact $t_{i-1} \sim_i t_i$ happens to be true, but the argument for it, *justification*$_i$, is wrong. We consider a calculation to be a proof that we write in order to convince ourself and others that a certain fact is true. The proof will not be convincing if there is a step without a valid justification. This highlights the important distinction between something being true and us knowing that something is true. In mathematics, we do not have any other way of knowing that a proposition is true than by proving it. If our proof has holes in it, then we know nothing about the proposition. Only when the whole proof is correct do we know that the proposition is true.

2.7 Assignments

1. Simplify $a^{x+3} \cdot a^{x-2} \cdot \left(a^{-x-1}\right)^2$ (assume $a \neq 0$).
2. Solve the equation $5x - 2(x - 1) = 2$.
3. Solve the equation $x^2 + 5x - 24 = 0$.
4. Solve the equation $x^3 - 6\frac{1}{2}x^2 - 3\frac{1}{2}x = 0$.
5. Calculate $\int_0^\pi (\sin(x) + \cos(x))\,dx$.
6. Calculate $\frac{d}{dx}\left(x^2 \cos(2x)\right)$.
7. Solve the simultaneous equations $y = 2x - 3$ and $5x = -2y + 39$.
8. Prove $(\sin(x) + \cos(x))^2 - 1 = \sin(2x)$.
9. Solve the absolute value equation $|2x - 8| = 16$.
10. Prove that the equation $5 \cdot (2 - x) - 9 = 6 \cdot (3 - x) - (16 - x)$ is not satisfied for any values of the variable.

Chapter 3

Basic Tasks

A structured calculation describes the solution to a mathematical problem. A *structured task* extends structured calculations, so that we also write down the problem that we are solving, together with the solution to the problem. The solution will typically involve some kind of structured calculation.

A structured task starts with a request, stating what we are supposed to do. This request is really a question that we are asked to answer. This is followed by a calculation to find an answer to the question. We rewrite our introductory example as a structured task.

Example 8. Calculate the value of the expression $3 \cdot 2^3 + 4 \cdot 3^2 - 2 \cdot 4^2$.

- • What is the value of expression $3 \cdot 2^3 + 4 \cdot 3^2 - 2 \cdot 4^2$
- ⊩ {transitivity}
  $3 \cdot 2^3 + 4 \cdot 3^2 - 2 \cdot 4^2$
- = {calculate the powers}
  $3 \cdot 8 + 4 \cdot 9 - 2 \cdot 16$
- = {perform the multiplications}
  $24 + 36 - 32$
- = {perform the addition}
  $60 - 32$
- = {perform the subtraction}
  28
- □ The value is 28 ∎

3. BASIC TASKS

We write the question after the bullet, in the second column. We write the answer after the square, also in the second column. The justification after the "⊩" symbol explains why the answer is correct. Here we justify the answer with the fact that equality is transitive. The special symbols in a structured derivation can be given more intuitive names in the context of a task: "•" is *task*, "□" is *answer*, and "⊩" is *conclusion*.

We are usually asked to solve a task under some given *assumptions*. The assumptions are listed after the question, writing "-" in the first column for each assumption. The question and the assumptions together form the *problem* that we are to solve. The following is an example of a task with assumptions.

Example 9. Calculate the value of the expression $3 \cdot x^3 + 4 \cdot y^2 - 2 \cdot 4^2$, when $x = 2$ and $y = 3$.

- •   What is the value of the expression $3 \cdot x^3 + 4 \cdot y^2 - 2 \cdot 4^2$, when
- - $x = 2$, and
- - $y = 3$
- ⊩   {transitivity}

  $3 \cdot x^3 + 4 \cdot y^2 - 2 \cdot 4^2$
- =   {insert the values x and y from the assumptions}

  $3 \cdot 2^3 + 4 \cdot 3^2 - 2 \cdot 4^2$
- =   {calculate the powers}

  $3 \cdot 8 + 4 \cdot 9 - 2 \cdot 16$
- =   {perform the multiplications}

  $24 + 36 - 32$
- =   {perform the addition}

  $60 - 32$
- =   {perform the subtraction}

  28
- □   The value is 28

Here the conclusion is that the answer 28 follows from the calculation steps by transitivity. ∎

An assumption is a logical proposition (a logical statement), i.e., a statement that is either true or false, depending on the values we assign to the variables in the statement. We identify an assumption by writing "-" in the first column. Alternatively, we can use numbers or lower case letters in parentheses, like in (a), (b), (c),..., to identify assumptions, so that we can refer to specific assumptions in the justifications.

One of the things that mathematicians really hate is to write down redundant information. They prefer brevity and elegance over precise details. The idea is that "an intelligent reader" can fill in the missing details. On the other hand, the basic idea of structured derivations is to make this implicit, hidden information explicit in mathematical arguments. There is a clear conflict between these two goals. We will solve this problem by allowing *default* information in a derivation: a derivation with missing information stands for a complete derivation where the missing information has been replaced by defaults.

The previous task is an example where we could be more brief. We could omit the answer after the "□" symbol, because it just repeats the last line of the calculation. We may also omit the justification for why this answer is correct, because it is the standard one, i.e., transitivity. In other words,

- the *default answer* is the last line of the calculation, and
- the *default justification* for the answer is transitivity.

We use these defaults in the sequel whenever they are applicable, to make the derivation more concise. Using these defaults in the example above gives us a slightly more compressed derivation.

Example 10. Solving same problem as above, but using defaults.

•	What is the value of the expression $3 \cdot x^3 + 4 \cdot y^2 - 2 \cdot 4^2$, when
-	$x = 2$, and
-	$y = 3$
⊩	$3 \cdot x^3 + 4 \cdot y^2 - 2 \cdot 4^2$
=	{insert the values x and y from the assumptions}
	$3 \cdot 2^3 + 4 \cdot 3^2 - 2 \cdot 4^2$
=	{calculate the powers}
	$3 \cdot 8 + 4 \cdot 9 - 2 \cdot 16$
=	{perform the multiplications}
	$24 + 36 - 32$
=	{perform the addition}
	$60 - 32$

3. Basic Tasks

$\quad=\quad${perform the subtraction}

$\qquad 28$

☐

Note that we move the first line of the calculation up one step, to the place where the justification of the answer is written, to save space. ■

Example 11. Simplify $\cos(x + \frac{\pi}{3})$ when $\sin x = \cos x$.

- Simplify $\cos(x + \frac{\pi}{3})$, when
- $\sin x = \cos x$

$\Vdash\quad \cos(x + \frac{\pi}{3})$

$\quad=\quad${the angle sum formula: $\cos(a+b) = \cos a \cdot \cos b - \sin a \cdot \sin b$}

$\qquad \cos x \cdot \cos \frac{\pi}{3} - \sin x \cdot \sin \frac{\pi}{3}$

$\quad=\quad${insert values: $\sin \frac{\pi}{3} = \frac{\sqrt{3}}{2}$ and $\cos \frac{\pi}{3} = \frac{1}{2}$}

$\qquad \frac{1}{2} \cos x - \frac{\sqrt{3}}{2} \sin x$

$\quad=\quad${by the assumption}

$\qquad \frac{1}{2} \cos x - \frac{\sqrt{3}}{2} \cos x$

$\quad=\quad${factor out $\cos x$}

$\qquad \frac{1-\sqrt{3}}{2} \cos x$

☐

The assumption implies that $\cos x = \pm \frac{1}{\sqrt{2}}$, so we could in fact carry out the simplification even further, to get the answer $\pm \frac{1-\sqrt{3}}{2\sqrt{2}}$. We will later show how to use this kind of observations in calculations. ■

We add another example of a task, now from analysis.

Example 12. Derive a formula for the derivative of the product of two functions f and g, when both f and g are differentiable.

The product of functions $f : \mathbb{R} \to \mathbb{R}$ and $g : \mathbb{R} \to \mathbb{R}$, denote $fg : \mathbb{R} \to \mathbb{R}$, is defined by
$$(fg)(x) = f(x) \cdot g(x)$$
for every $x \in \mathbb{R}$.

- Calculate $(fg)'(x)$, when

(a) f and g are differentiable

(b) $(fg)(x) = f(x) \cdot g(x)$, for every $x \in \mathbb{R}$

⊩ $(fg)'(x)$

=   {the definition of derivative}

$$\lim_{h \to 0} \frac{(fg)(x+h) - (fg)(x)}{h}$$

=   {the definition of product function}

$$\lim_{h \to 0} \frac{f(x+h)g(x+h) - f(x)g(x)}{h}$$

=   {we can add $f(x)g(x+h) - g(x+h)f(x)$ to the numerator, since the value of this expression is 0}

$$\lim_{h \to 0} \frac{f(x+h)g(x+h) - f(x)g(x) + f(x)g(x+h) - g(x+h)f(x)}{h}$$

=   {regroup the numerator}

$$\lim_{h \to 0} \frac{f(x+h)g(x+h) - g(x+h)f(x) + f(x)g(x+h) - f(x)g(x)}{h}$$

=   {the first two terms have the common factor $g(x+h)$ and the last two terms have the common factor $f(x)$}

$$\lim_{h \to 0} \frac{g(x+h)(f(x+h) - f(x)) + f(x)(g(x+h) - g(x))}{h}$$

=   {we split the expression into two separate sums}

$$\lim_{h \to 0} \left(\frac{g(x+h)(f(x+h) - f(x))}{h} + \frac{f(x)(g(x+h) - g(x))}{h} \right)$$

=   {we calculate the limits separately for the two terms}

$$\lim_{h \to 0} \frac{g(x+h)(f(x+h) - f(x))}{h} + \lim_{h \to 0} \frac{f(x)(g(x+h) - g(x))}{h}$$

=   {rewrite the expressions}

$$\lim_{h \to 0} g(x+h) \frac{f(x+h) - f(x)}{h} + \lim_{h \to 0} f(x) \frac{g(x+h) - g(x)}{h}$$

=   {when $h \to 0$, the fractional expressions approach $f'(x)$ and $g'(x)$, and $g(x+h) \to g(x)$}

$$g(x)f'(x) + f(x)g'(x)$$

□   ■

3. Basic Tasks

3.1 Questions and Answers

A task starts with a question: what values will satisfy some given condition. Examples of questions are:

What values of the variable x satisfy the condition $x^2 + 2x + 1 = 0$ (solving an equation)?

What values of the variables x and y satisfy the conditions that $2x+y = 3$ and $3x - y = 4$ (simultaneous equations)?

What is a simpler form for the expression $s = \dfrac{x^2 - 1}{x + 1}$ (simplification)?

What is the value of $a = \sin(2\pi)^2$ (calculating a value)?

Tasks are often not phrased as questions but rather as requests: "Solve the equation...", "Simplify the expression...", "Calculate the value of...". But behind a request is a question that we want to answer. The answer is then a logical proposition that shows which values satisfy the condition.

We have two kinds of basic questions that we may ask in a task. Sometimes we want to find *all* values that satisfy a given condition (e.g., when solving an equation), while in other cases we are looking for *some* value that satisfies the condition (e.g., in simplification). It is also important to specify the domain where we search for acceptable values. We also need to state whether we are looking for values for a single variable, or whether we are looking for values for two or more variables at the same time.

The general form for a *some-question*

$$? \, x_1 : A_1, \ldots, x_m : A_m : Q(x_1, \ldots, x_m)$$

and for an *all-question*

$$! \, x_1 : A_1, \ldots, x_m : A_m : Q(x_1, \ldots, x_m)$$

Here $x_1, \ldots, x_m$ are the variables for which we want to find suitable values, and $A_1, \ldots, A_m$ are the value domains for these variables. We consider $x : A$ as an alternative notation for $x \in A$. This means that we are looking for values $x_1 \in A_1$, $x_2 \in A_2$ and so on. A list of the form $x_1 : A_1, \ldots, x_m : A_m$ is known as a *declaration*. The purpose of a declaration is to introduce new names for variables (and constants) and associate a value domain with each of these new names.

The logical proposition $Q(x_1, \ldots, x_m)$ describes the conditions that the values for $x_1, \ldots, x_m$ must satisfy. We write "?" when we are looking for **some** values for $x_1, \ldots, x_m$ that satisfy $Q(x_1, \ldots, x_m)$, and "!" when we are looking for **all** values for $x_1, \ldots, x_m$ that satisfy $Q(x_1, \ldots, x_m)$.

The answer to a some-question will be of the form $(x_1, \ldots, x_m) = (t_1, \ldots, t_m)$. The answer to an all-question will be another logical proposition $R(x_1, \ldots, x_m)$ from which it is easy to see the values that satisfy the original proposition.

Example 13. Some example questions:

1. Solve the equation $x^2 + 2x + 1 = 0$:
   $$!\,x : \mathbb{R} :\ x^2 + 2x + 1 = 0$$
   In other words, find **all** values $x \in \mathbb{R}$ that satisfy the equation $x^2 + 2x + 1 = 0$. The answer could be of the form "$x = e_1 \vee x = e_2$" (here "$\vee$" stands for "or").

2. Solve the equation pair
   $$\begin{cases} 2x + y = 3 \\ 3x - y = 4 \end{cases}$$
   This can be expressed as the question
   $$!\,x : \mathbb{R},\ y : \mathbb{R} :\ 2x + y = 3 \wedge 3x - y = 4$$
   ("$\wedge$" stands for "and"). In other words, we want to find **all** value combinations (x, y) that satisfy the two equations, $2x + y = 3$ and $3x - y = 4$. The answer could be of the form "$x = e_1 \wedge y = e_2$".

3. Simplify the expression $\dfrac{x^2 - 1}{x + 1}$. This can be expressed as the question
   $$?\,s : \mathbb{R} :\ s = \frac{x^2 - 1}{x + 1}$$
   Here we want to find some value (or expression) s that is equal to the original expression, but simpler in some way. What it means to be simpler depends on the context, and the rules are not always that explicit. The answer could be of the form "$s = e$".

4. Solve the equation $\frac{1}{2} = \sin x^2$. This can be expressed as the question
   $$!\,x : \mathbb{R} :\ \frac{1}{2} = \sin x^2$$
   The equation has an infinite number of solutions x, because the sine function is periodic. We are looking for an expression that characterizes all these solutions. The answer would then be a logical proposition that shows all possible values of x that satisfy the equation.

5. Prove that $(x + y)^2 = x^2 + 2xy + y^2$. Here we are not looking for any values for variables, we just want to prove that the equation holds for any values of x and y. We can phrase this as the question with an empty variable list,
   $$?\ (x + y)^2 = x^2 + 2xy + y^2$$
   We are asked to prove a proposition for which the answer is also given, i.e., that the proposition is true. Our task is to just fill in the proof that shows that this answer is correct. ∎

3. BASIC TASKS

We often place additional constraints on what answers are acceptable. A solution to an equation may only allow propositions where x is on the left-hand side of an equality. When we simplify an expression, we might allow only certain operations in the simplified expression. Sometimes the answer must be exact, sometimes an approximation is sufficient. We will not elaborate here on what kind of restrictions we may have on the answer, as this is very dependent on the type of problem that we are solving.

The rules for what is an accepted answers to a question are often not very explicit, and depend on what we need the answer for. Simplification of an expression is a good example of this. If the task is to simplify the expression $10 \cdot \sqrt{\frac{12}{5}}$, then the answer we are looking for is probably $4 \cdot \sqrt{15}$. This is the simplest form of the original expression, because it has no fraction and the expression under the square root cannot be simplified further. The answer is correct, because $10 \cdot \sqrt{\frac{12}{5}} = 4 \cdot \sqrt{15}$. However, from a purely logical point of view, the answer $10 \cdot \sqrt{\frac{12}{5}}$ is equally correct, because $10 \cdot \sqrt{\frac{12}{5}} = 10 \cdot \sqrt{\frac{12}{5}}$ is also true. In other words, even if an answer is correct in the sense that we have defined above, it may still not be the answer we are looking for, because we place some additional (extra-logical) requirements on the answer we want to have.

We will in the sequel follow standard mathematical practice and express the task as a request rather than as a question. However, it is important to understand that the task is really a question, and that the purpose of the task is to find an answer to this question. With a little experience, it becomes quite easy to see the implied question in a request, and thus what kind of answer we should be looking for.

3.2 Proof Tasks

A *proof task* is the simplest form of a task. In this case, we do not need to determine any variable values, we only want to prove that a given proposition is true.

Example 14. The following is an example of a proof task.

- Show that $(1+a)(1+b)(1+c) \geq 1+a+b+c$, when
- $a, b, c \geq 0$

The solution (the proof) is given below:

⊩   {transitivity of equality}

      $(1+a)(1+b)(1+c)$

=   {expand the last two parentheses}

      $(1+a)(1+b+c+bc)$

3.2. Proof Tasks

$=$ {expand the remaining two parentheses}

$1 + b + c + bc + a + ab + ac + abc$

$\geq$ {$ab + ac + bc + abc$ is non-negative, since a, b, and c are all positive, according to the assumption}

$1 + a + b + c$

$\square$ ■

We can interpret the square here as the completion of the proof ("Quad erat demonstrandum", "Which had to be proven", often abbreviated as Q.E.D.)

The proof task is correct, if all calculation steps are correct, and the proposition Q that we want to prove follows from the assumptions and the calculation steps. To be more precise, consider a proof task of the general form

- Q
- Φ

$\Vdash$ $justification_0$

t_0

$\sim_1$ $justification_1$

t_1

$\vdots$

$\sim_k$ $justification_k$

t_k

$\square$

Here Φ stands for the list of assumptions in the proof task. We are asked to prove that the proposition Q follows from the assumptions Φ in the task. The proof may be carried out in some external context Φ_0. Correctness of the proof task is defined as follows.

Definition 2. The proof task above is *correct* in the external context Φ_0, if

(a) the calculation is correct in the context of Φ_0 and Φ, and

3. BASIC TASKS

(b) *justification*$_0$ proves Q in the context of Φ_0, Φ, and the calculation steps $t_0 \sim_1 t_1, \ldots, t_{k-1} \sim_k t_k$. [1] ∎

The justifications in the task may thus refer to any properties in the external context Φ_0 (like a general mathematical theorem), to the specific assumptions Φ in the task, and to the calculation steps in the task. In the example above, the justification "transitivity of equality" refers to all the calculation steps in the solution. The external context could, e.g., state that the constants a, b and c stand for real values, and could include the general properties of multiplication, addition, and comparison of real numbers.

3.3 Calculation Tasks

A *calculation task* is a task where we only show the calculation, leaving the question, the answer and the justification for the answer implicit. There are also no explicit assumptions in a calculation task, any assumptions we need must be stated in the context of the task. In spite of this, the calculation task is very useful. Our previous trigonometry example, written as a calculation task, is shown below.

Example 15. Simplify $\cos(x + \frac{\pi}{3})$ when we know that $\sin x = \cos x$. We solve the task directly by calculating:

- $\cos(x + \frac{\pi}{3})$

$=$ {the angle sum formula: $\cos(a + b) = \cos a \cdot \cos b - \sin a \cdot \sin b$}

$\cos x \cos \frac{\pi}{3} - \sin x \sin \frac{\pi}{3}$

$\vdots$

$=$ {factor out $\cos x$}

$\frac{1-\sqrt{3}}{2} \cos x$

□

This calculation is carried out in a context where the assumption $\sin x = \cos x$ is known to hold. The default task is "simplify the expression on the first line of the calculation". The default answer is given by the expressions on the last line, and the default justification is transitivity. ∎

---

[1] Condition (b) can be written as

$$\Phi_0, \Phi, t_0 \sim_1 t_1, \ldots, t_{k-1} \sim_k t_k \vdash Q \text{ by } justification_0$$

using the notation introduced earlier.

3.4 Is the Answer Correct

How do we check that the answer we get in a task is correct? We have two kinds of questions in a task, some-questions (looking for some answers) and all-questions (looking for all answers). We consider these two separately.

A task with a some-question has the general form shown below:

- $?\,x : A : Q(x)$
- Φ
- ⊩ *justification*
- ⋮ (calculation)
- □ $x = t$

Here Φ stands for the sequence of assumptions in the task, and t is some expression.

Once we have found the answer, we need to check whether the answer is correct. Correctness depends on two things: are all the calculation steps correct, and have we given the right answer to the question based on the calculation steps.

The answer $x = t$ is right, if the answer t is in the required value domain ($t \in A$), and if it satisfies the condition stated in the question ($Q(t)$). Consider Example 11 above. Here the problem was to simplify $\cos(x + \frac{\pi}{3})$. We can formulate this as the question

$$?\,s : \mathbb{R} : \cos(x + \frac{\pi}{3}) = s$$

The answer we gave was that $s = \frac{1-\sqrt{3}}{2}\cos x$. The first condition, $t \in A$, is the requirement that $\frac{1-\sqrt{3}}{2}\cos x \in \mathbb{R}$, which obviously is the case. The second condition, $Q(t)$, is the requirement that

$$\cos(x + \frac{\pi}{3}) = \frac{1-\sqrt{3}}{2}\cos x$$

(we get this by substituting the answer $\frac{1-\sqrt{3}}{2}\cos x$ for s in the question). The second condition follows from the calculation steps and transitivity.

Definition 3. We say that the *answer* $x = t$ to the some-question $?\,x : A : Q(x)$ *is correct* when $t \in A$ and $Q(t)$. ∎

Let us next consider a task with an all-question. A typical example is, e.g., solving an equation. Consider solving the equation $7x^2 - 6x = 0$. The following task solves this problem:

3. BASIC TASKS

- $!x : \mathbb{R}:\ 7x^2 - 6x = 0$
- ⊩ {equivalence is transitive}
  $7x^2 - 6x = 0$
- ≡ {the distributive law: $ab + ac = a(b+c)$}
  $x(7x - 6) = 0$
- ≡ {the rule of zero product: $ab = 0 \equiv (a = 0 \vee b = 0)$}
  $x = 0 \vee 7x - 6 = 0$
- ≡ {solve the equation in the RHS disjunct}
  $x = 0 \vee x = \frac{6}{7}$
- □ $x = 0 \vee x = \frac{6}{7}$

The solution to the quadratic equation is given as a disjunction, i.e., the answer $R(x)$ is a $x = 0 \vee x = \frac{6}{7}$. The answer is correct, because

$$(7x^2 - 6x = 0) \equiv (x = 0 \vee x = \frac{6}{7})$$

The equivalence shows that $(x = 0 \vee x = \frac{6}{7}) \Rightarrow (7x^2 - 6x = 0)$, i.e., that both $x = 0$ and $x = \frac{6}{7}$ are solutions to the equation, and that $(7x^2 - 6x = 0) \Rightarrow (x = 0 \vee x = \frac{6}{7})$, i.e., that a solution to the equation is either $x = 0$ or $x = \frac{6}{7}$. In other words, $(x = 0 \vee x = \frac{6}{7})$ describes all solutions to the equation.

The general form of a task with an all-question is

- $!x : A : Q(x)$
- $-$ Φ
- ⊩ *justification*
- ⋮ (calculation)
- □ $R(x)$

Here Φ again stands for the assumptions in the task, and $R(x)$ is a logical statement that describes all possible solution values x.

When is the answer $R(x)$ correct? We obviously have to require that $R(x) \Rightarrow Q(x)$ holds, i.e., that any answer x satisfies the condition $Q(x)$ in the question. This means that we do not have any false answers. On the other hand, we also require that we have all the answers, i.e., $Q(x) \Rightarrow R(x)$, so that any value x that satisfies the condition $Q(x)$ is among the answers. Combining these two gives us the condition $R(x) \equiv Q(x)$ for the answer to be correct. From this follows that

$$\{x \mid R(x)\} = \{x \mid Q(x)\}$$

The set of values in the answer is thus the same as the set of values that satisfy the question condition.

Definition 4. We say that the answer $R(x)$ to the all-question $!x : A : Q(x)$ is *correct* when $R(x) \equiv Q(x)$ for every $x \in A$. ∎

We can now define what it means for a task to be correct. Consider the following general task:

- •   *question*
- - Φ
- ⊩   *justification*
- ⋮   (calculation)
- □   *answer*

Definition 5. A task above is *correct* in the external context Φ_0, if

(a) the calculation is correct in the context of Φ_0 and the assumptions Φ of the task, and

(b) *justification* proves that *answer* is correct in the context of Φ_0, Φ, and the calculation steps.

∎

3.5   A More Verbal Format

Structured tasks contain special symbols that identify the different parts of the task, like "•", "‖ " and "□". Formalizing the notation for tasks is similar to what has happened in mathematics in general: the "+" symbol was introduced as a shorthand for writing "the sum of..." and the "=" symbol was introduced as a shorthand for saying that two expressions have the same value. Introducing special symbols for important mathematical concepts shortens the writing, but also paves the way for a universal mathematical language and provides an unambiguous interpretation of these symbols. In our case, this means that a task looks the same in every language and that a task has an unambiguous logical interpretations.

When teaching structured derivations for the first time, it may be easier for students to understand a structured task by first using traditional words instead of symbols.

3. BASIC TASKS

Example 16. We can rewrite Example 14 in a more verbose notation, e.g., like this:

Question:	Is the statement $(1+a)(1+b)(1+c) \geq 1+a+b+c$ always true
Assumption:	$a, b, c \geq 0$
Conclusion:	{the answer follows from the calculation below}
	$(1+a)(1+b)(1+c)$
=	{expand the last two parentheses}
	$(1+a)(1+b+c+bc)$
=	{expand the remaining two parentheses}
	$1+b+c+bc+a+ab+ac+abc$
$\geq$	{$ab+ac+bc+abc$ is non-negative, since $a,b,c \geq 0$, according to the assumption}
	$1+a+b+c$
Answer:	The statement is true

∎

The verbal form is more intuitive, but at the same time it gives the impression that the task is an informal description of a problem and its solution, and that it is open to different interpretations. This, however, is not the case, a structured derivation has a logical meaning that is as exact as, e.g., the value of an arithmetic expression. We will stick to the more concise symbolic notation for tasks in the rest of the book, but teachers are free to use the verbal form when they feel that it makes it easier to understand the task and its solution.

We can also have an intermediate form, where the main steps of the calculation are described in more verbose notation, while the details are described symbolically. We will give some examples of this later on.

3.6 Assignments

1. Solve the equation $(x-5) - x = \frac{9}{x}$.
2. Solve the equation $\frac{x+7}{x} - 9 = \frac{x-3}{2x}$.
3. Solve the equation $(x+1)^2 - 3 = \frac{3x^2}{x+1}$.
4. Solve the equation $x \ln(x) - x = 0$, $x > 0$.
5. Is $x = -\frac{5}{\sqrt{2}}$ a solution to the equation $\sqrt{3}x - \sqrt{2}x = 5 + 9^{\frac{1}{4}}x$?

6. Prove that the value of the expression $\dfrac{\log\left(b^2\right) - \log\left(\sqrt[5]{b^2}\right)}{\log\left(\sqrt{b}\right) - \log\left(b^{\frac{1}{3}}\right)}$ is independent of the value of the parameter b, where $b > 0$ and $b \neq 1$.

7. Determine the limit $\lim\limits_{x \to 3} \dfrac{\ln\left(x^3\right) - \ln\left(27\right)}{\ln\left(x\right) - \ln\left(3\right)}$.

8. Prove that the sequence $a_n = \dfrac{n!}{n^n}$ is strictly decreasing, when $n = 1, 2, 3, \ldots$

9. Define the *double factorial* for even numbers as $(2n)!! = 2n \cdot (2n-2) \cdot \ldots \cdot 2$,, when $n = 1, 2, 3, \ldots$ and $0!! = 1$. Rewrite the double factorial $(2n)!!$ in terms of the regular factorial $n!$.

CHAPTER **4**

General Tasks

Basic tasks are for situations where we just state the problem and then solve it with a single calculation. For more complex problems, it can be difficult to see how to solve the problem directly. Rather, we have to construct a solution one step at a time. Starting from the assumptions, we make a series of *observations*, until we have enough information to solve the main problem, with or without a final calculation. We have two different kinds of observations, *facts* that follow from the assumptions, and *definitions* for introducing new concepts.

We also have another way of breaking up a larger task into smaller, more manageable tasks: *subtasks* or *nested tasks*. We will show below how to extend the basic tasks that we described above with these three modularization methods.

4.1 Facts

A *fact* consists of two parts: the justification that explains why the fact follows from the assumptions and earlier observations, and the fact itself. A "+" symbol, or a number or small letter in square brackets ([1], [2],...), identifies this as a fact. The justification is written on a line of its own, before the fact itself. The general format for a fact is shown below on the left, while an example of a fact is shown on the right.

fact		
+ *justification*	+	{by assumption (b)}
proposition		$2 \leq x$

The example states that $2 \leq x$ follows directly from some assumption (b).

Example 17. Nadja and Peter each rent a car for one day. Nadja pays 50 € per day, plus 0.40 € per km. Peter rents a car from another company that charges 70

4. GENERAL TASKS

€ per day and 0.30 € per km. How many kilometers should Nadja and Peter drive so that they pay the same rent for their cars.

First we identify the question and the assumptions of the problem:

- How many kilometers x should Nadja and Peter drive, to make their cost of renting the cars equal, when

(a) Nadja pays 50 € per day and 0.40 € per km.

(b) Peter pays 70 € per day and 0.30 € per km.

(c) Nadja and Peter rent their cars for one day

Next we observe some facts that follow directly from the assumptions:

[1] {We see from assumptions (a) and (c) what Nadja pays}

Nadja pays $50 + 0.40 \cdot x$ euros to drive x km

[2] {We see from assumptions (b) and (c) what Peter pays}

Peter pays $70 + 0.30 \cdot x$ euros to drive x km.

We now calculate the answer by writing an equation and solving it:

$\Vdash$ {we solve the equation below for x}

Nadja pays as much as Peter for driving x kilometers

$\equiv$ {observation [1] and [2]}

$$50 + 0.40 \cdot x = 70 + 0.30 \cdot x$$

$\equiv$ {regroup the terms}

$$0.40 \cdot x - 0.30 \cdot x = 70 - 50$$

$\equiv$ {simplify}

$$0.10 \cdot x = 20$$

$\equiv$ {divide by 0.10}

$$x = \frac{20}{0.10}$$

$\equiv$ {calculate}

$$x = 200$$

$\square$ Peter and Nadja should both drive 200 km

The task has thus been solved: Nadja and Peter pay the same rent if they drive 200 km. ∎

Notice that we mix lines from the structured task with text that explain how we solve the task. This is useful for longer tasks with more complex solutions. The informal text can explain the strategy we use for solving the assignment, or the intuition behind the observations, or show us how to interpret the answer. In addition to text, we can also have figures, illustrations, tables, graphs, etc. Mixing prose and displayed formulas is standard in mathematical for longer arguments, and is also useful for structured derivations.

We distinguish between the structured derivation and explaining text by indenting each line of the derivation one step to the right. This is similar to how we display equations on a separate line in a standard mathematical presentation. The difference is that the equation is centered on the line, while the derivation is left justified and indented.

Example 18. A dart board has a radius of 20 cm, and it is divided into ten rings of uniform width, numbered from 1 to 10 (starting from the outside). Gabriel hits the dart board so that the distance r (in cm) from the center of the board is distributed according to the density function

$$f(r) = \begin{cases} \dfrac{3}{16000}(400 - r^2), & \text{when } 0 \leq r \leq 20 \\ 0, & \text{else} \end{cases}$$

Calculate the probability that Gabriel scores a 9 or a 10.

We start by formulating the problem.

- Calculate the probability that the dart hits 9 or 10, when

(a) the radius of the dart board is 20 cm

(b) each ring has the same width, and

(c) the density function is $f(r) = \begin{cases} \dfrac{3}{16000}(400 - r^2), & \text{when } 0 \leq r \leq 20 \\ 0, & \text{else} \end{cases}$, where r is the distance from the center of the board to the dart

The dart board looks like this:

4. GENERAL TASKS

The figure allows us to make the following observation.

[1]   {follows from assumptions (a) and (b)}

the dart hits 9 or 10 if, and only if, $0 \leq r \leq 4$.

We are now ready to calculate the solution to the problem.

⊩ P(Gabriel hits 9 or 10)

=   {observation [1]}

$P(0 \leq r \leq 4)$

= $\{P(A) = \int_c^d f(x)\,dx$, the interval of integration is given by [1]$\}$

$\int_0^4 f(r)\,dr$

= $\{f(r)$ is given by assumption (c) $\}$

$\int_0^4 \dfrac{3}{16000}(400 - r^2)\,dr$

=   {integrate using formula $\int (f(x) + g(x))\,dx = \int f(x)\,dx + \int g(x)\,dx$}

---
[1]Picture by Kallerna

$$\int_0^4 \frac{3}{16000} \cdot 400 \, dr - \int_0^4 \frac{3}{16000} \cdot r^2 \, dr$$

$= \quad$ {integrate using formula $\int_a^b cx^n \, dx = \left[c \cdot \frac{x^{n+1}}{n+1}\right]_a^b$}

$$\left[\frac{3 \cdot 400}{16000} r\right]_0^4 - \left[\frac{3r^3}{3 \cdot 16000}\right]_0^4$$

$= \quad$ {simplify}

$$\left[\frac{3}{40} r\right]_0^4 - \left[\frac{r^3}{16000}\right]_0^4$$

$= \quad$ $\{[F(x)]_a^b = F(b) - F(a)\}$

$$\frac{3}{40} \cdot 4 - \frac{3}{40} \cdot 0 - \frac{64}{16000} + \frac{0}{16000}$$

$\approx \quad$ {calculate an approximative value}

0.3

$\square \quad$ $P(\text{Gabriel hits 9 or 10}) \approx 0.3$. ∎

4.2 Definitions

It is often useful to introduce new notations in proofs and derivations, e.g., to simplify a calculation by introducing a name for a complex subexpression. We do this using *definitions*. Below is the general format for a definition. On the right, we have an example of a definition:

<u>*definition*</u>

$+ \quad$ *decl* $\qquad\qquad + \quad c : \mathbb{R}$

$\qquad$ *justification* $\qquad\qquad \{a \neq 0$, so c is well-defined$\}$

$\qquad$ *proposition* $\qquad\qquad c = \frac{e^a - 1}{a}$

The definition is written in three lines. The first line *declares* the name of the constant and its value domain. The second line is a justification that explains why the constant is well-defined. The third line gives the condition that defines the constant. Note that the name of the constant must be new, we are not allowed to reuse an existing name for the definition.

The name of the constant is c in the example, and the value domain is $\mathbb{R}$. The definition condition is

$$c = \frac{e^a - 1}{a}$$

4. GENERAL TASKS

The justification explains why c is well-defined, i.e., that there is value in the value domain that satisfies the definition condition. In this case, the constant c is well-defined when $a \neq 0$. We can then use c freely in the rest of the derivation, and replace c by its definition $\dfrac{e^a - 1}{a}$ whenever needed.

Sometimes we need to introduce two or more constants at the same time. We can also make the definition more compact by writing the constant declaration and the justification on the same line. Below is the format for this more compact notation. On the right we have a typical case when we need to define two or more constants at the same time. We say that a real number a is rational, if it can be written as a fraction $\dfrac{p}{q}$, where p and q are two integers. The right hand side below shows a definition that introduces p and q.

definition

+   *decl   justification*   + $p, q : \mathbb{Z}$ {a is a rational number}

     proposition $a = \dfrac{p}{q}$

Note that this is an *implicit definition* of the constants p and q, it does not stipulate a unique value for these two numbers. For $a = \frac{1}{3}$, we could choose $p = 1$ and $q = 3$, but we could as well choose $p = 6$ and $q = 18$ or $p = 201$ and $q = 603$.

Example 19. Three siblings inherit 12 000 € in total. The inheritance is to be split among the sibling in the ratio 5:3:2. How large a share will each sibling get?

- How large are the shares A, B and C of the inheritance, when

(a)   the inheritance is 12 000, and

(b) A, B and C split the inheritance in the ratio 5:3:2

[1]   {assumptions (a) and (b)}

$A + B + C = 12\,000$

We introduce a constant a that allows us to express the shares of each heir.

[2] $a : \mathbb{R}$ {a well-defined because of assumption (b)}

$A = 5a \land B = 3a \land C = 2a$

⊩ $A + B + C = 12\,000 \land A = 5a \land B = 3a \land C = 2a$

≡   {substitute the values of A, B and C}

$$5a + 3a + 2a = 12\,000 \wedge A = 5a \wedge B = 3a \wedge C = 2a$$

$\equiv$ {solve the equation}

$$a = 1\,200 \wedge A = 5a \wedge B = 3a \wedge C = 2a$$

$\Rightarrow$ {property of the conjunction}

$$A = 6\,000 \wedge B = 3\,600 \wedge C = 2\,400$$

☐ A gets $6\,000$, B gets $3\,600$ and C gets $2\,400$

The last step uses implication instead of equivalence. This is because we omit the condition for a in the last expression, as we do not need it. The implication does not hold in the opposite direction, the last expression does not say anything about the value of a so the two propositions are not equivalent. ∎

4.3 Correctness of Observations

Consider a task with observations, of the form

-    *question*
-    Φ

[1] $x_1 : A_1$ {*justification*$_1$}

      P_1

$\vdots$

[n] $x_n : A_n$ {*justification*$_n$}

      P_n

⊩   *justification*$_0$

$\vdots$ (calculation)

☐   *answer*

Here $x_i : A_i$ is missing when $[i]$ is a fact.

Definition 6. Consider the task with observations above, in the external context Φ_0. *Observation $[i]$* is *correct* in this task, if

(a) the observation is a fact, and *justification$_i$* proves proposition P_i in the context of Φ_0, Φ, and $P_1, \ldots, P_{i-1}$, or

(b) the observation is a definition, and *justification$_i$* proves that there exists a value for x_i that belongs to A_i and satisfies proposition P_i, in the context of Φ_0, Φ, and $P_1, \ldots, P_{i-1}$.

We say that the *observations* in the task are *correct* in context Φ_0 and Φ, if all observations are correct in this context. ∎

In other words, if step $[i]$ is a fact, then we need to prove that this fact follows from the external context, the task assumptions and the previous observations. If step $[i]$ is a definition, we need to show that the constant is well-defined, in the same context.

4.4 Solving Problems as Tasks

We describe the solution to a mathematical problem in the form of a structured task. But this does not mean that we have to construct the solution step-by-step in the same order as the different components of the task are enumerated in the final solution. We often approach a problem in ways that later turn out to be unsuccessful, we sometimes change the question or the assumptions, and we may make them more precise. We can make irrelevant observations, or identify additional assumptions at a later stage that we did not notice earlier, etc. We need to write the components of a structured task in a particular order to avoid circular reasoning, but this order does not have to be the one we follow when we work out the problem and look for a solution.

Solving a math problem is to some extent analogous to solving programing problems. First we need to find a strategy for solving the problem, and then work out the details. Some of the details are straightforward, while others can be very tricky. A structured task is comparable to a program, it is the format we use to write down the final solution to the problem. While we are working on the problem, a structured task functions as repository for facts and information that we discover during the process. This allows us to work step by step towards a final solution of the problem.

A computer based editor for structured derivation is very useful here, since we can then easily make changes to the task, add some components, remove others as wrong or unnecessary, and copy expressions from one line to another. This is more cumbersome when we work with pen and paper: scribblings, deletions and corrections in the text. And, we may need to rewrite the final solution from start to end to hand in a clean text.

We show below how one can use structured derivations as a support structure when solving a problem. Once we have solved the problem, we have a systematic presentation of the problem and its final solution.

Example 20. Prove that $m^2 - n^2 \geq 3$, when m and n are positive natural numbers and $m > n$.

4.4. Solving Problems as Tasks

We start by working out the problem: what should we do (the question) and which assumptions are we allowed to make. In this case, the problem is as follows:

- Prove that $m^2 - n^2 \geq 3$, when
(a) $m : \mathbb{N}, m > 0$
(b) $n : \mathbb{N}, n > 0$
(c) $m > n$

We want to prove that the statement is true. We start by simplify the expression $m^2 - n^2$. We immediately notice that we can use the conjugate rule here. After adding this step, the task looks as follows (red text indicate what is new):

- Prove that $m^2 - n^2 \geq 3$, when
(a) $m : \mathbb{N}, m > 0$
(b) $n : \mathbb{N}, n > 0$
(c) $m > n$

$\Vdash$ $\{\}$

$m^2 - n^2$

$=$ $\{$by the conjugate rule$\}$

$(m-n)(m+n)$

The curly bracket for justifying the answer is still empty, since we have not solved the problem yet.

We now notice that we can use the monotonicity of a product, i.e., that $ab \geq ab'$, if $a \geq 0$ and $b \geq b'$. We can use this rule to prove $(m-n)(m+n) \geq (m-n) \cdot 3$, if we can show that $m - n \geq 0$ and $m + n \geq 3$. We show this by adding two facts before the calculation. The task now look as follows, with the new addition now shown in red:

- Prove that $m^2 - n^2 \geq 3$, when
(a) $m : \mathbb{N}, m > 0$
(b) $n : \mathbb{N}, n > 0$
(c) $m > n$

[1] $\{$(c) implies that $m - n > 0$, so $m - n \geq 1\}$

$m - n \geq 1$

4. GENERAL TASKS

[2]   {(a) - (c) imply that $n \geq 1$ and $m \geq n+1 \geq 2$, so $m+n \geq 3$}

     $m + n \geq 3$

⊩   {}

     $m^2 - n^2$

=   {by the conjugate rule}

     $(m-n)(m+n)$

≥   {the product is monotonic: $ab \geq ab'$, when $a \geq 0$ and $b \geq b'$. [1] and [2]}

     $(m-n) \cdot 3$

We complete the task by applying the same rule once more, now for expression $(m-n) \cdot 3$, to get the final solution.

- Prove that $m^2 - n^2 \geq 3$, when

(a) $m : \mathbb{N}$, $m > 0$

(b) $n : \mathbb{N}$, $n > 0$

(c) $m > n$

[1]   {from (c) follows that $m - n > 0$, so $m - n \geq 1$}

     $m - n \geq 1$

[2]   {from (a) - (c) follows that $n \geq 1$ and $m \geq n + 1 \geq 2$, so $m + n \geq 3$}

     $m + n \geq 3$

⊩   {the statement follows from the transitivity of $\geq$}

     $m^2 - n^2$

=   {by the conjugate rule}

     $(m-n)(m+n)$

≥   {the product is monotonic: $ab \geq ab'$, when $a \geq 0$ and $b \geq b'$, [1] and [2]}

     $(m-n) \cdot 3$

≥   {the product is monotonic, observation [1]}

     $1 \cdot 3$

=   {arithmetics}

     3

□

The example shows that the task was not constructed in the same order as it is written down in the final solution. We have inserted observations at the beginning when we needed them. We have also added justifications later, when we saw what they should be.

4.5 Nested Tasks

Structured calculations require that each step in the calculation is explicitly justified. In many cases, it is sufficient to write a comment in angular brackets as a justification, as we have done in the examples we have described until now. There are, however, many situations where a simple explanation is not sufficient, but we would really need to do another calculation in order to see that the step is correct. We refer to such sub-calculations as *nested calculation tasks*. Consider as an example the following calculation problem and its solution.

Example 21. Calculate the value of the expression $2 + (3 \cdot 2^3 + 4 \cdot 3^2) \cdot 2 \cdot 4^2 - 2 \cdot 5^2$

- $2 + (3 \cdot 2^3 + 4 \cdot 3^2) \cdot 2 \cdot 4^2 - 2 \cdot 5^2$
= {calculate the powers in the parenthesis}
  $2 + (3 \cdot 8 + 4 \cdot 9) \cdot 2 \cdot 4^2 - 2 \cdot 5^2$
= {multiply in the parenthesis}
  $2 + (24 + 36) \cdot 2 \cdot 4^2 - 2 \cdot 5^2$
= {add in the parenthesis}
  $2 + 60 \cdot 2 \cdot 4^2 - 2 \cdot 5^2$
= {calculate the powers in the entire expression}
  $2 + 60 \cdot 2 \cdot 16 - 2 \cdot 25$
= {multiply}
  $2 + 1920 - 50$
= {add and subtract}
  1872

□ ■

The expression in parentheses has to be evaluated first, before the main calculation. The problem with the calculation above is that we have to copy the part of the expression that lies outside the parenthesis from one line to another when we manipulate the expression inside the parenthesis. This is redundant, since this part does not change from one line to the next, and it is error prone, particularly if we

4. GENERAL TASKS

do this by hand. For long and complex expressions, it also becomes difficult to see which part of the expression is being manipulated from one step to another.

Nested calculations solve this problem. A nested calculation is a structured calculation that is carried out as part of a larger structured task. We can add a nested calculation to any justification, to give a more detailed explanation for the derivation step. A nested calculation is a separate calculation that supports the justification. The nested calculation is indented on step to the right. The next example shows the previous calculation written with a nested calculation

Example 22. Example of a structured task with a nested calculation.

-     $2 + (3 \cdot 2^3 + 4 \cdot 3^2) \cdot 2 \cdot 4^2 - 2 \cdot 5^2$
- $=$ {calculate the value inside the parenthesis}

  -     $3 \cdot 2^3 + 4 \cdot 3^2$
  - $=$ {calculate the powers}
  -     $3 \cdot 8 + 4 \cdot 9$
  - $=$ {multiply}
  -     $24 + 36$
  - $=$ {add}
  -     60

  □

- $\ldots$ $2 + 60 \cdot 2 \cdot 4^2 - 2 \cdot 5^2$
- $=$ {calculate the powers in the entire expression}
-     $2 + 60 \cdot 2 \cdot 16 - 2 \cdot 25$
- $=$ {multiply}
-     $2 + 1920 - 50$
- $=$ {add and subtract}
-     1872

□   ■

The three dots in the left column after the nested calculation shows where the main calculation continues. This will give us more lines in the derivation, but we have to type fewer characters, since we do not have to copy expressions that remain unchanged from one line to the next. The nested calculation also shows clearly which part of the expression is being manipulated.

Using a computer to write structured derivations can again be quite useful here. An *outlining editor*, i.e., an editor that can selectively show and hide indented text,

4.5. Nested Tasks

is particularly useful. We can then hide the nested calculation when we want to concentrate on the overall solution, and show the nested calculation again when we want to check the details. Hiding the nested calculation in the previous calculation gives us the following derivation:

- $\quad 2 + (3 \cdot 2^3 + 4 \cdot 3^2) \cdot 2 \cdot 4^2 - 2 \cdot 5^2$
= $\quad$ {calculate the parenthesis}
... $\quad 2 + 60 \cdot 2 \cdot 4^2 - 2 \cdot 5^2$
= $\quad$ {calculate the powers in the entire expression}
$\quad 2 + 60 \cdot 2 \cdot 16 - 2 \cdot 25$
= $\quad$ {multiply}
$\quad 2 + 1920 - 50$
= $\quad$ {add and subtract}
$\quad 1872$

☐

The three dots now show that the first justification contains a hidden nested calculation. ∎

The following example shows a more substantial example of how to organize and simplify the calculation of arithmetic expressions.

Example 23. Simplify the expression $\sqrt{7 + 2\sqrt{11}} + \sqrt{7 - 2\sqrt{11}}$

Our approach is to square the expression, then simplify it and finally take the square root of the simplified expression.

- $\quad$ Simplify the expression $\sqrt{7 + 2\sqrt{11}} + \sqrt{7 - 2\sqrt{11}}$
⊢ $\quad \sqrt{7 + 2\sqrt{11}} + \sqrt{7 - 2\sqrt{11}}$
= $\quad$ {we square the expression, simplify it and then insert the square root of the simplified expression}

  - $\quad (\sqrt{7 + 2\sqrt{11}} + \sqrt{7 - 2\sqrt{11}})^2$
  = $\quad$ {the square rule}
  $\quad 7 + 2\sqrt{11} + 2 \cdot \sqrt{7 + 2\sqrt{11}} \cdot \sqrt{7 - 2\sqrt{11}} + 7 - 2\sqrt{11}$
  = $\quad$ {simplify}
  $\quad 14 + 2 \cdot \sqrt{7 + 2\sqrt{11}} \cdot \sqrt{7 - 2\sqrt{11}}$
  = $\quad$ {focus on the second subexpression $2 \cdot \sqrt{7 + 2\sqrt{11}} \cdot \sqrt{7 - 2\sqrt{11}}$}

4. GENERAL TASKS

- $2 \cdot \sqrt{7 + 2\sqrt{11}} \cdot \sqrt{7 - 2\sqrt{11}}$
= {the product of two radicals}
  $2 \cdot \sqrt{(7 + 2\sqrt{11}) \cdot (7 - 2\sqrt{11})}$
= {the conjugate rule}
  $2\sqrt{49 - 4 \cdot 11}$
= {simplify}
  $2\sqrt{5}$
□

... $14 + 2\sqrt{5}$
□

... $\sqrt{14 + 2\sqrt{5}}$

□ The simplified expression is $\sqrt{14 + 2\sqrt{5}}$.

We use two nested derivations here, one inside the other. The original problem is to simplify a sum of square roots. Instead of doing this directly, we simplify the square of this expression in a nested derivation. The square root of the simplified expression is then the solution to our original problem. Inside the first nested derivation, we then carry out a separate nested derivation, where we simplify a part of the complex square expression. Focusing on a part of the expression in the nested derivation makes it easier to see what we manipulate in the derivation. There will also be fewer errors, as we avoid copying long expressions from line to line. ∎

We can use nesting for arbitrary tasks, not only for calculation tasks. We rewrite our earlier number theory example to use *nested tasks*.

Example 24. Prove that $m^2 - n^2 \geq 3$, when m and n are positive integers, and $m > n$.

- Prove that $m^2 - n^2 \geq 3$, when
(a) m is a positive integer,
(b) n is a positive integer, and
(c) $m > n$

⊩ $m^2 - n^2$
= {by the conjugate rule}
  $(m - n)(m + n)$
≥ {the product is monotonic: $ab' \geq ab$, when $a \geq 0$ and $b' \geq b$}
  - $m - n$
  > {assumption (c)}

$$
\begin{array}{rl}
= & n - n \\
 & \{\text{arithmetics}\} \\
 & 0 \\
\square & \\
\bullet & m + n \\
\geq & \{\text{assumption (c)}\} \\
 & n + 1 + n \\
\geq & \{\text{assumption (b)}\} \\
 & 1 + 1 + 1 \\
= & \{\text{arithmetics}\} \\
 & 3 \\
\square & \\
\ldots & (m - n) \cdot 3 \\
\geq & \{\text{the product is monotonic, } m - n > 0 \text{ according to (c), and } 3 \geq 0\} \\
 & 1 \cdot 3 \\
= & \{\text{arithmetics}\} \\
 & 3 \\
\square &
\end{array}
$$

The second calculation step uses two nested tasks, to show that the two constraints for applying the rule are both satisfied. We have the same situation in the third step, but now it is easier to see that the constraints are satisfied, so we handle this without nested derivations. ∎

4.6 Inheritance

The use of nested tasks can greatly simplify a structured derivation, by dividing the overall problem into smaller and more manageable subproblems. The nested tasks are solved in the context of the justification that they support. This means that all assumptions, facts and definitions that are available at the point where the justification is written are also available in the nested tasks for that justification. In other words, the nested tasks *inherit* the assumptions, facts and definitions of their justification. Therefore, we need not repeat these in the nested tasks.

This inheritance is clearly shown in Example 24. The first nested task uses assumption (c), which is given on the outer level. The second nested task uses both assumptions (c) and (b) from the outer level. Generally, a nested task can refer to any preceding assumptions, observations and definitions at an outer level compared to the nested task and written before this task. We are not allowed to refer to assumptions or observations that are made after the nested task, regardless of what level they are on. This restriction prevents circular reasoning when solving a task.

4.7 General Syntax for Tasks

The general format for structured tasks is shown in the following template:

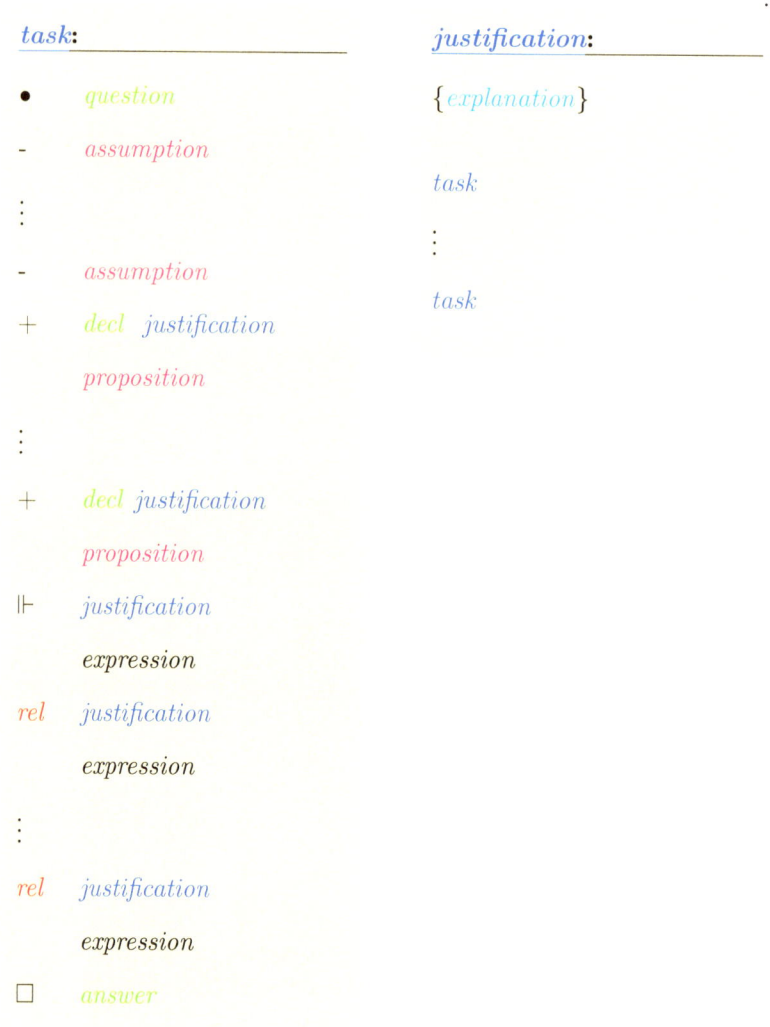

This template shows that tasks are *recursive* in nature:

- Each step in a structured task comes with a justification.
- A justification can again contain nested tasks.

The nested tasks inside a justification may have their own justifications, which again may contain nested tasks, and so on. The recursion ends with a justification that does not introduce any new nested tasks.

4.7. General Syntax for Tasks

We emphasize the recursive structure of tasks by coloring tasks and justifications blue. The other components of a structured derivation are colored in other colors, depending on their type: the question and answer are colored green, logical propositions are colored magenta, relations are colored red, justification explanations are colored cyan, while expressions and declarations are colored black.

We illustrate the general syntax for tasks with an example that we have given earlier (Example 20). This task has 3 assumptions, 2 observations and 4 calculation steps. We have chosen to identify the assumptions by letters and the observations by numbers, so that we can refer to them individually in the derivation.

•	*question*	•		Prove that $m^2 - n^2 \geq 3$, when
(a)	*assumption*	(a)		$m : \mathbb{N}, m > 0$
(b)	*assumption*	(b)		$n : \mathbb{N}, n > 0$
(c)	*assumption*	(c)		$m > n$
[1]	*justification*	[1]		{ (c) implies that $m - n > 0$, so $m - n \geq 1$ }
	proposition			$m - n \geq 1$
[2]	*justification*	[2]		{ (a) - (c) imply $n \geq 1$ and $m \geq n + 1 \geq 2$ }
	proposition			$m + n \geq 3$
⊩	*justification*	⊩		{ follows from the transitivity of $\leq$ }
	expression			$m^2 - n^2$
rel	*justification*		=	{by the conjugate rule}
	expression			$(m - n)(m + n)$
rel	*justification*		$\geq$	{product is monotonic, observation [1] and [2]}
	expression			$(m - n) \cdot 3$
rel	*justification*		$\geq$	{ product is monotonic, observation [1]}
	expression			$1 \cdot 3$
rel	*justification*		=	{arithmetics}
	expression			3
☐	*answer*	☐		the proposition is true

Note that *justifications* on the left are colored blue, because they stand for general justifications, which may have nested derivations. In the example on the right, each justification is of the simple form *{explanation}*, and is hence colored cyan. We will

4. General Tasks

postpone the discussion on the correctness of tasks with nested tasks to Chapter 7.

4.8 Assignments

1. Solve the simultaneous equations
$$x = 5 \land y = x + 12 \land z = 2x + y - 2z$$

2. Solve the simultaneous equations
$$2z + y - 2x = 6\frac{1}{3} \land 10y - x = \frac{z}{18} \land z + 2 = 2x + 2\frac{1}{3} - y$$

3. Solve the absolute value equation $|2x - 8| = 3x - 5$.

4. Solve the inequality $2x^2 + 20x + 32 > 0$.

5. Solve the absolute value equation $|x^3 - x^2 + 2x - 2| = 4x^2 + 8$.

6. The points $A = (-4, -6, 0)$ and $B = (5, 3, 1)$ are in the same plane. Can the vector $\bar{n} = -49\bar{i} + 51\bar{j} - 18\bar{k}$ be a normal vector to the plane?

7. A line passes through the point $(4, 2, 1)$ and is directed along the vector $2\bar{i} + 3\bar{j} - \frac{5}{3}\bar{k}$. Determine if the line intersects the xy-plane and if so, where it intersects it.

8. When appending the digits 91 to the end of a specific integer we get the original number multiplied by 107. What is the original number?

# Chapter 5

Problem Solving Paradigms

There are essentially three main paradigms for solving mathematical problems: *calculations*, *forward derivations*, and *backward derivations*. We will show how each of these paradigms can be formulated as a structured task, and then show how a structured task allows us to combine all three paradigms in a single derivation.

We will illustrate each paradigm by proving the same simple theorem, each time following a different paradigm. Finally we give a proof that combines two of these paradigms in a structured task. The problem we consider is the following:

> Prove that $k^2 + k$ is an even number when k is a natural number.

5.1 Calculations

Calculation are central tools in all of mathematics, in particular in science and engineering. A standard calculation would not contain observations or nested tasks, and the conclusion is usually implicit.

Example 25. We prove our example theorem with a calculation. We do this by calculating the truth value of the statement that $k^2 + k$ is even, and find that it is true.

- Show that $k^2 + k$ is even, when
- $k : \mathbb{N}$
- ⊩ $k^2 + k$ is even
- ≡ {write the expression as a product}
-   $k(k+1)$ is even
- ≡ {a product is even if and only if one of the factors is even}
-   k is even or $k+1$ is even

5. Problem Solving Paradigms

≡   {every second natural number is even, so either k or $k+1$ must be even}

   $true$

□

The calculation shows that the original statement is equivalent to true for any natural number, which means that the statement is true. ∎

A structured task that is solved with a calculation would have the following general form:

- •   *question*
-    *assumption*
  ⋮
-    *assumption*
- ⊩   *expression*
- rel   {*explanation*}
       expression
  ⋮
- rel   {*explanation*}
       expression
- □   *answer*

5.2 Forward Derivations

A forward derivation is a proof that starts from given facts (the assumptions) and then adds one observation after the other, until we reach an observation that proves the theorem that we are interested in. Each observation is shown to follow from the assumptions and previous observations. This proof method was introduced by the greek mathematicians, and resulted in, e.g., the impressive treatment of Euclidean geometry.

There are no calculations in a forward derivation, and the arguments are simple, i. e., there are no nested tasks. The assumptions and observations are numbered, so that that we can refer to them when justifying the observations.

Example 26. We prove our example theorem with a forward derivation.

5.2. Forward Derivations

- Show that $k^2 + k$ is even, when
- $k \in \mathbb{N}$

[1] {each natural number is either even or odd}

  k is even or k is odd

[2] {a natural number is odd iff the next number is even, observation [1]}

  k is even or $k + 1$ is even

[3] {a product of two natural numbers is even if one of the numbers is even, observation [2]}

  $k \cdot (k + 1)$ is even

[4] {distribution rule: $k \cdot (k + 1) = k^2 + k$, observation [3]}

  $k^2 + k$ is even

⊩ {the theorem follows from observation [4]}

□ ■

A structured task that is solved with forward derivations would look as follows:

- *question*

(a) *assumption*

  ⋮

(m) *assumption*

[1] {*explanation*}

  proposition

  ⋮

[n] {*explanation*}

  proposition

⊩ {*explanation*}

□ *answer*

5. Problem Solving Paradigms

5.3 Backward Derivations

A task solved with backward derivations would not include any calculations nor any forward derivation. Instead, we use justifications with nested tasks. The basic idea is that solving the main problem is reduced to solving a number of simpler sub-problems (nested tasks).

Example 27. We prove our example theorem with backward derivation. We will do this in stages. The problem that we want to solve is the following:

- Show that $k^2 + k$ is even, when
- k is a natural number

We first we reduce this task to two simpler tasks (marked with red) using case analysis.

- Show that $k^2 + k$ is even, when
- k is a natural number
⊩ {case analysis, consider the cases that k is even and that k is odd separately}

  - Show that $k^2 + k$ is even, when
  - k is an even number
  - Show that $k^2 + k$ is even, when
  - k is an odd number

□

The original problem has been reduced to two smaller problems: showing that the original statement is true when k is even, and showing that the statement is true when k is odd. As k must be either even or odd, it is sufficient to prove that the theorem holds in both these cases.

We now complete this proof with arguments that show that the two new theorems are true. We prove these two theorems without any further reductions. The new parts are again written in red.

- Show that $k^2 + k$ is even, when
- k is a natural number
⊩ { case analysis, consider the two cases that k is even and that k is odd separately}

  - Show that $k^2 + k$ is even, when
  - k is an even number

⊩ $\{k^2+k$ can be written as $k(k+1)$; k is even, so $k(k+1)$ is even$\}$
☐

- Show that k^2+k is even, when
- k is an odd number

⊩ $\{k^2+k$ can be written as $k(k+1)$; k is odd, so $k+1$ is even, so $k(k+1)$ is even$\}$
☐

☐

The recursion stops at the first level of nesting, because the nested tasks are proved directly, without introducing any new nested tasks. ∎

The general form for a task that we solve with backward derivations is as follows:

- *question*
- *assumption*
  ⋮
- *assumption*

⊩ $\{explanation\}$

     task
     ⋮
     task

☐   *answer*

We have here substituted the definition of justification directly in the task. A task now only states the question and the assumptions, together with a justification for why the answer is correct. This justification is, however, based on solving a number of other, nested tasks. These new tasks are then either solved directly, or reduced to further subtasks.

5.4 Combining Paradigms

The classical proof paradigms each have their strengths. Algebraic and numeric problems are best solved with calculations, complex mathematical problems are usually solved with forward derivations, while backward reduction is often the fastest way to find a proof, and is often used in computer based theorem proving. Structured

5. PROBLEM SOLVING PARADIGMS

tasks allow us to combine all these proof paradigms in a single general paradigm. We can, e.g., start by reducing the original problem to a number of simpler subproblems. We can then use calculations to solve some of the subproblems, observations for some other subproblems, and use further reductions for the remaining problems. Or, we can solve the original problem by combining observations, calculations and reductions in a single task. In essence, this means that we use the proof paradigm that is best suited for the problem and subproblem at hand.

Example 28. We prove that $k^2 + k$ is an even number for any natural number k, by combining backward proofs with calculations.

- Show that $k^2 + k$ is even, when
- k is a natural number
- ⊩ {case analysis, consider the two cases, k is even and k is odd}

    - Show that $k^2 + k$ is even, when
    - k is an even number
    - ⊩ $k^2 + k$ is even
    - ≡   {write as product}

      $k(k+1)$ is even
    - ⇐   {a product is even if one of the factors is even}

      k is even
    - ≡   {assumption}

      $true$
    - ☐

    - Show that $k^2 + k$ is even, when
    - k is an odd number
    - ⊩ $k^2 + k$ is even
    - ≡   {write as product}

      $k(k+1)$ is even
    - ⇐   {a product is even if one of the factors is even}

      $k+1$ is even
    - ≡   {number theory}

      k is odd
    - ≡   {assumption}

      $true$
    - ☐

☐

Note the use of backward implication in both nested tasks. We have in both cases showed that the desired result (that $k^2 + k$ is even) follows from the assumption made in the subtask. ■

Structured tasks thus combine the three main proof paradigms in a single new proof format. The sequence of assumptions and observations can be seen as a forward derivation, while the justification can be seen as a backward derivation. We can summarize the overall syntax of structured task in the following way, to show more clearly how the three proof paradigms are combined.

task	*justification*
• question	
forward derivation	{*explanation*}
	task
⊩ *justification*	⋮
calculation	
□ *answer*	*task*

The conclusion sign "⊩" separates the three proof paradigms from each other.

5.5 Examples

We give here a few examples that illustrate the power of combining proof paradigms in problem solving with structured derivations. Our first example is taken from analytic geometry.

Example 29. Find the point on the parabola $y = x^2 - 2x - 3$ where its tangent has the direction angle $45°$.

- Find the point (x, y) on the parabola f, where
(a) $f(x) = x^2 - 2x - 3$ for all $x \in \mathbb{R}$, and
(b) the tangent of the parabola at point (x, y) has direction angle $\alpha = 45°$
[1] {find the first derivative at point x}
  - the tangent of the parabola at point (x, y) has direction angle $45°$
  ≡ {the slope is $\tan \alpha$}
  the tangent of the parabola at point (x, y) has slope $\tan 45°$
  ≡ {$\tan 45° = 1$}
  the tangent of the parabola at point (x, y) has slope 1

5. Problem Solving Paradigms

$\equiv$ {the first derivative gives the slope}
$$f'(x) = 1$$
□

... $f'(x) = 1$

[2] {find x}

- $f'(x) = 1$
$\equiv$ {assumption (a), the derivative of f at the point x is $f'(x) = 2x - 2$}
$$2x - 2 = 1$$
$\equiv$ {solve for x}
$$x = \frac{3}{2}$$
□

... $x = \frac{3}{2}$

⊩ (x, y)
= {observation [2]}
$(\frac{3}{2}, y)$
= {assumption (a) and observation [2]}
$(\frac{3}{2}, (\frac{3}{2})^2 - 2(\frac{3}{2}) - 3)$
= {calculating}
$(\frac{3}{2}, -\frac{15}{4})$
□ $(x, y) = (\frac{3}{2}, -\frac{15}{4})$ ■

Now consider a problem in geometry.

Example 30. The length of two sides of a triangle are 5 and 11. The height to the third side splits that side in ratio $3 : 7$. Calculate the length of the unknown side.

We draw a figure to illustrate the problem. We have labeled the sides (a, b and c) and the height (h).

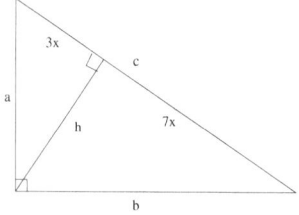

5.5. Examples

Let us formulate the problem:

- Calculate c, when
  - 5, 11 and c are (the lengths of the) sides of a triangle
  - h is the height against the side c, and
  - h splits c in a ratio $3 : 7$

We introduce x as one tenth of c, so that we can describe the two parts of c as $3x$ and $7x$.

[1] $x : \mathbb{R}$ {define x as tenth of c}

$c = 10x$

We can use the Pythagorean theorem for two different right triangles:

[2]   {Pythagorean theorem for the triangle with sides h, $3x$ and 5}

$h^2 + 9x^2 = 25$

[3]   {Pythagorean theorem for the triangle with sides h, $7x$ and 11}

$h^2 + 49x^2 = 121$

We can now solve x from observations [2] and [3]

[4]   {calculate x}

- [2] and [3]
- $\equiv$ {write down the observations}

  $h^2 + 9x^2 = 25$ and $h^2 + 49x^2 = 121$
- $\Rightarrow$ {subtract the first equation from the second and simplify}

  $40x^2 = 96$
- $\equiv$ {divide both sides by 40 and simplify}

  $x^2 = \frac{12}{5}$
- $\equiv$ {take the square root of both sides, note that $x > 0$}

  $x = \sqrt{\frac{12}{5}}$
- □

... $x = \sqrt{\frac{12}{5}}$

We are now ready to calculate c.

5. Problem Solving Paradigms

$\Vdash \quad c$

$= \quad$ {definition [1]}

$\quad 10x$

$= \quad$ {observation [4]}

$\quad 10 \cdot \sqrt{\frac{12}{5}}$

$= \quad$ {extend by 5 under the root}

$\quad 10 \cdot \sqrt{\frac{60}{25}}$

$= \quad$ {extend by 5 under the root and simplify}

$\quad 10 \cdot \dfrac{2 \cdot \sqrt{15}}{5}$

$= \quad$ {simplify}

$\quad 4 \cdot \sqrt{15}$

$\square \quad c = 4 \cdot \sqrt{15}$ ∎

The next example shows how to solve a problem involving series.

Example 31. Calculate the sum of the geometric series

$$a + ar + ar^2 + \ldots + ar^{n-1}$$

for $n \geq 1$, when $r \neq 1$ and $r \neq 0$.

We start by formulating the problem:

- Calculate $a + ar + ar^2 + \ldots + ar^{n-1}$, when
- $r : \mathbb{R}$, $r \neq 0$ and $r \neq 1$, and
- $n : \mathbb{N}$, $n \geq 1$

We introduce an auxiliary constant, s, that turns out to be very useful for solving the problem.

[1] $\quad s : \mathbb{R}$ {since $r \neq 0$, the expression r^{n-1} is defined for $n = 1$ (note that 0^0 is undefined), hence s is defined for $n \geq 1$}

$\quad s = 1 + r + r^2 + \ldots + r^{n-1}$

Next, we make two observations about s. Both observations make use of nested calculations.

[2]   {calculate $s - rs$}

- $s - rs$
= {the definition of s, calculate rs}
$1 + r + r^2 + \ldots + r^{n-1} - (r + r^2 + r^3 + \ldots + r^n)$
= {simplify}
$1 - r^n$
□

... $s - rs = 1 - r^n$

[3]   {find s by solving the equation in [2]}

- $s - rs = 1 - r^n$
≡ {factor out s}
$s(1 - r) = 1 - r^n$
≡ {divide by $1 - r$, allowed because $r \neq 1$ by assumption}
$s = \frac{1-r^n}{1-r}$
□

... $s = \frac{1-r^n}{1-r}$

Finally, we are ready to solve the original problem

⊩ $a + ar + ar^2 + \ldots + ar^{n-1}$
=   {factor out a}
$a \cdot (1 + r + r^2 + \ldots + r^{n-1})$
=   {definition [1]}
as
=   {observation [3]}
$a\frac{1-r^n}{1-r}$
□ $a + ar + ar^2 + \ldots + ar^{n-1} = a\frac{1-r^n}{1-r}$ ■

Our final example shows how to solve a problem in geometry that involves the use of figures and geometric constructions.

Example 32. We give here one of the classical proofs of the Pythagorean Theorem. The proof is based on a sequence of geometric constructions. The geometric constructions are shown here in a succession of figures, where the initial situation (the right triangle) is colored green, the first extension is colored orange and the second extension is colored blue.

5. Problem Solving Paradigms

- (*The Pythagorean Theorem*) Show that $a^2 + b^2 = c^2$, where

(a) c is the hypotenuse of a right triangle and a and b are the legs of the triangle.

We thus have the following initial situation:

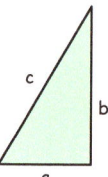

Our first step is to draw a square on the hypotenuse.

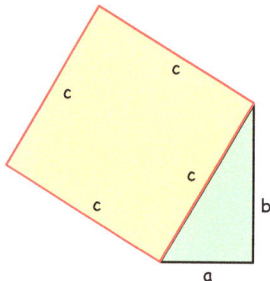

[1] $A_{small} : \mathbb{R}$ $\{c > 0$, so small square is well-defined$\}$

A_{small} is the area of the square drawn on the hypothenuse

[2] $\{$area of square$\}$

$A_{small} = c^2$

Then we draw three copies of the original right triangles around the square, so that the legs a and b are co-linear and coincide at each corner. The four triangles and the small square then form a larger square

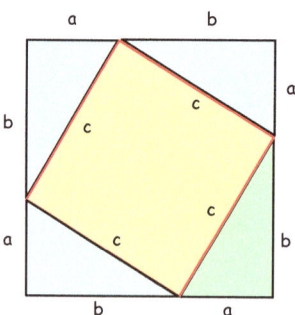

[3] $A_{large} : \mathbb{R}$ {the large square is well-defined by the construction}

   A_{large} is the area of the square formed by the small square and the four right triangles.

[4]   {area of a square}

   $A_{large} = (a+b)^2$

[5] $A_{triangle} : \mathbb{R}$ {area of the original right triangle}

   $A_{triangle}$ is the area of the original triangle

[6]   {area of right triangle}

   $A_{triangle} = \dfrac{a \cdot b}{2}$

[7]   {calculate the area of the small square A_{small} using the areas of the large square and the triangle}

- A_{small}
= {the small square is the difference between the large square and the four triangles}
  $A_{large} - 4 \cdot A_{triangle}$
= {inserting A_{large} and $A_{triangle}$ from the observations [4] and [6]}
  $(a+b)^2 - 4 \cdot \dfrac{a \cdot b}{2}$
= {using the square rule and simplifying the last term}
  $a^2 + 2 \cdot a \cdot b + b^2 - 2 \cdot a \cdot b$
= {simplify}
  $a^2 + b^2$

□

... $A_{small} = a^2 + b^2$

⊦   {observations [2] and [7] show that $a^2 + b^2 = c^2$}

□   ■

5.6 Assignments

1. Prove that there exists three consecutive natural numbers whose sum is 171.

2. Prove that $x^3 - x$ is divisible by 3, when $x \in \mathbb{N}$.

3. Determine when the expression $\sqrt{x^2 - 1} + \dfrac{\sqrt{10 - x^2}}{\sqrt{x - 2}}$ is defined.

4. Prove the logarithm rule $\log_a \frac{x}{y} = \log_a x - \log_a y$.

5. A line passes through the points $(5, 2, -1)$ and $(6, 4, -3)$. At which point does the line intersect the xz-plane?

6. Prove that the (generally false) formula $(x+y)^3 = x^3 + y^3$ only holds if $y = 0$, $x = 0$, both of the aforementioned or $x = -y$.

7. Provide an example of such numbers x and y that satisfy the (generally false) formula $(x-y)^3 = x^3 - y^3$, but not the formula from the previous task.

8. Prove that $\lg(25)$ is not a rational number.

CHAPTER 6

Word Problems

We have in previous chapters showed how to formulate and solve mathematical tasks. Let us now take a step back, and think about how to solve problems that arise in the real world with mathematics. In school mathematics, this kind of problems are known as *word problems*. We will here look at how to formulate word problems as tasks, and how to interpret the answers as solutions to the original problem.

6.1 Word Problems as Tasks

We can identify four distinct steps when solving a real-world problem:

1. We start by *analyzing* the *informal description* of the problem: what are the relevant quantities in the problem context, what is the question, and what assumptions are we allowed to make. We then reformulate the informal problem as a *mathematical problem*.

2. We then *solve* the mathematical problem to get a *mathematical answers* to the problem.

3. Next, we formulate a *solution* in the informal context of the original problem, based on the mathematical answer we have found.

4. Finally we *evaluate* the solution, to see whether it is a correct or at least a reasonable solution to the original problem.

We summarize this process in Figure 6.1. We can reiterate this process a number of times, as long as our evaluation shows that the answer is incorrect or implausible.

We rephrase this model in our framework as shown in Figure 6.2. The informal problem statement is first formulated as the problem of a task, with a question and assumptions. We then complete the task with observations and calculations that lead to an answer to the task question. Having found a mathematical answer, we interpret it in the context of the original problem, to get a solution to the problem. Finally, we try to check whether the solution is correct. If correctness is too difficult to check, we may at least try to see whether the solution is reasonable.

6. WORD PROBLEMS

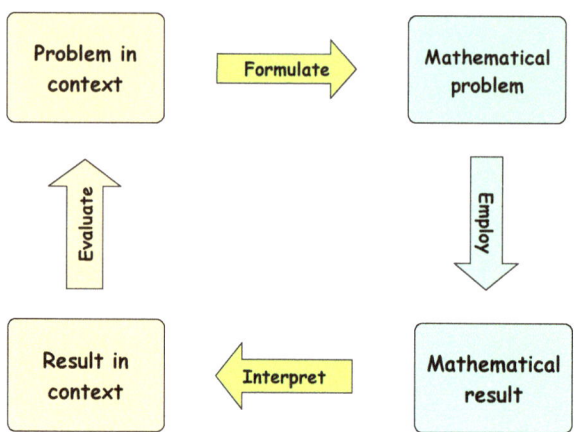

Figure 6.1: Solving real-world problems

A structured task does not, by itself, have any direct links to the problems in the real world that we are trying to solve. In practice, it is, however, important that we can show how the mathematical problem statement is related to the informal problem statement. We describe this relationship with *comments* that we add to a derivation. A comment is an arbitrary text which can be added to the end on any line in a derivation (in the second column), and is preceded with "—". The comment can continue into the next line (the second column). We can also have a line that only has a comment. The comments have no relevance for the solution of the mathematical problem, i.e., we can omit all comments without changing the meaning of the derivation. We see comments as something that is outside the actual syntax for structured derivations. A comment explains what the question, assumptions or answer of the task mean in the original context of the problem.

Example 33. A holiday package to Madeira consists of hotel and travel expenses. The cost of the hotel had decreased by 5% since last year, while the travel expenses have increased by 18%. The price of the entire package is still the same as last year. Calculate how many percentages of the total price of last year package went to travel expenses.

We start by formulating the problem mathematically. First we identify which entities appear in the problem. We introduce symbols for last year's hotel expenses (x) and last year's travel expenses (y), as well as this years hotel expenses (x') and this years travel expenses (y'). Then we can specify the task and the assumptions. The meaning of these entities are explained in comments. For clarity, we have colored all comments blue. We now have the following mathematical formulation of the problem:

- How many percent is y of $x + y$ — how many percent is last year's travel expenses of the entire holiday package last year

- $x : \mathbb{R}^+$ — last year's hotel expenses

6.1. Word Problems as Tasks

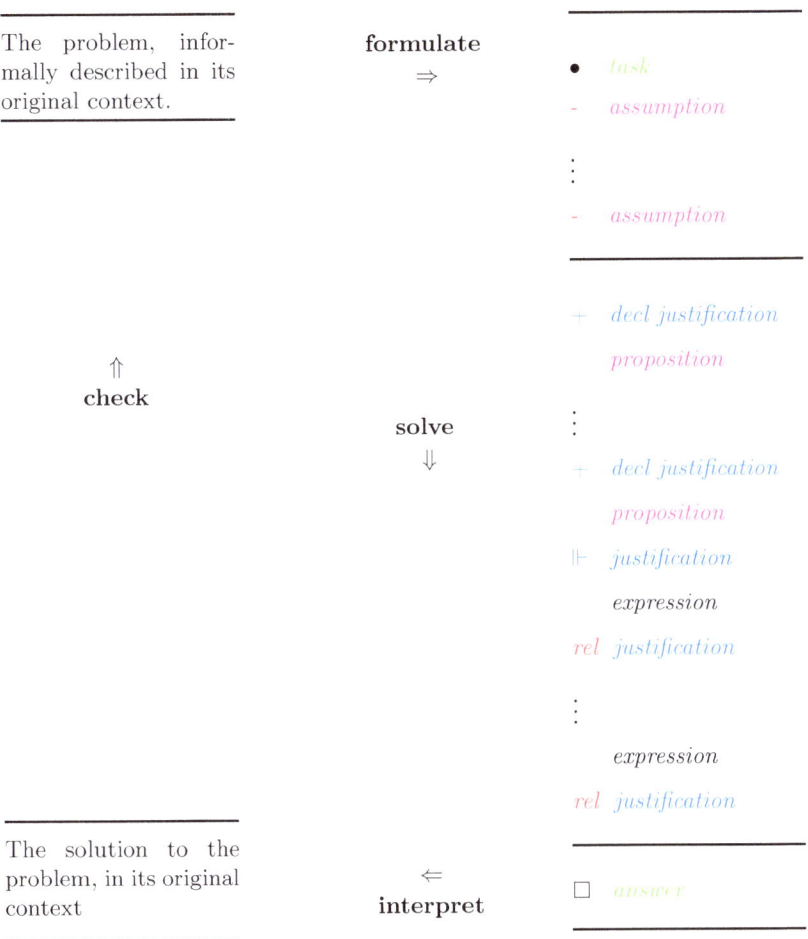

Figure 6.2: Modeling with a structured task

- $y : \mathbb{R}^+$ — last year's travel expenses
- $x' : \mathbb{R}^+$ — this year's hotel expenses
- $y' : \mathbb{R}^+$ — this year's travel expenses
(a) x' is 5 % less than x — this year's hotel expenses are 5 % less than last year
(b) y' is 18 % greater than y — this year's travel expenses are 18 % greater than last year
(c) $x' + y' = x + y$ — the price of the entire holiday package this year is the same as last year

The comments give the connection between the mathematical formulation of the problem and the original informal problem formulation. The quantities that we ob-

6. WORD PROBLEMS

serve are introduced as variable names, with assumptions about their value domain. These assumptions are not numbered, since we can refer to them directly by name.

Our first observation shows that we can describe this year's hotel and travel expenses using last year's hotel and travel expenses.

[1]   {we describe this year's hotel and travel expenses using last year's hotel and travel expenses, assumptions (a) and (b)}

$x' = 0.95x$ and $y' = 1.18y$

The next step is to use assumption (c), which says that the total cost this year is the same as last year.

[2]   {calculate y using assumption (c)}

-     $x + y = x' + y'$
- $\equiv$ {observation [1]}
-     $x + y = 0.95x + 1.18y$
- $\equiv$ {subtract x from both sides}
-     $y = -0.05x + 1.18y$
- $\equiv$ {subtract $1.18y$ from both sides}
-     $-0.18y = -0.05x$
- $\equiv$ {divide both sides by -0.18}
-     $y = \frac{0.05}{0.18}x$

□

... $y = \frac{5}{18}x$

We can now solve the original problem, i.e., calculate how many percent of the entire holiday package went towards travel expenses last year:

⊢ $\dfrac{y}{x+y}$

=   {observation [2]}

$\dfrac{\frac{5}{18}x}{x + \frac{5}{18}x}$

=   {cancel out x}

$\dfrac{\frac{5}{18}}{1 + \frac{5}{18}}$

=   {simplify}

6.1. Word Problems as Tasks

$$\frac{5}{23}$$

$\approx$ {calculate an approximate value}

0.2173913

$\approx$ {round and write as a percentage}

21.7%

☐ 21.7% — last years travel expenses were 21.7% of the entire holiday package

We have now an answer to the mathematical problem, 21.7%, which is also the solution to the original problem: last year's travel expenses were 21.7% of the entire holiday package.

Let us finally check if the answer is correct, or at least reasonable. We calculate the share of travel expenses this year.

• travel expenses share of total package this year

= {assumptions}

$$\frac{y'}{x' + y'}$$

= {assumption (c), observation [1]}

$$\frac{1.18y}{x+y}$$

= {observation [2]}

$$\frac{1.18x}{\frac{18}{5}y + y}$$

= {simplify}

$$\frac{5 \cdot 1.18}{23}$$

$\approx$ {calculate}

25.6%

☐

Since the total cost of the package is the same as last year, we see that the increase in travel expenses is

$$\frac{25.6 - 21.7}{21.7} \approx 18\%$$

Thus, our answer seems to be correct. ■

6. Word Problems

Example 34. Here is the same solution to the previous problem, but now using mnemonic names for the entities involved (in the programming language tradition). We remove the comments from this solution, as it is now easier to remember what the different propositions stand for.

- How many percent is last years travel costs (tra_{last}) of last years total holiday package, which consisted of hotel costs (hot_{last}) and travel cost.
  - $hot_{last} : \mathbb{R}^+$
  - $tra_{last} : \mathbb{R}^+$
  - $hot_{now} : \mathbb{R}^+$
  - $tra_{now} : \mathbb{R}^+$

(a) hot_{now} is 5 % less than hot_{last}

(b) tra_{now} is 18 % greater than tra_{last}

(c) $hot_{now} + tra_{now} = hot_{last} + tra_{last}$

[1] {we describe this year's hotel and travel expenses using last year's hotel and travel expenses, assumptions (a) and (b)}

$hot_{now} = 0.95 \cdot hot_{last}$ and $tra_{now} = 1.18 \cdot tra_{last}$

[2] {calculate tra_{last} using assumption (c)}

- $hot_{last} + tra_{last} = hot_{now} + tra_{now}$
- $\equiv$ {observation [1]}
  $hot_{last} + tra_{last} = 0.95 \cdot hot_{last} + 1.18 \cdot tra_{last}$
- $\equiv$ {subtract hot_{last} from both sides}
  $tra_{last} = -0.05 \cdot hot_{last} + 1.18 tra_{last}$
- $\equiv$ {subtract $1.18 \cdot tra_{last}$ from both sides}
  $-0.18 \cdot tra_{last} = -0.05 \cdot hot_{last}$
- $\equiv$ {divide both sides by -0.18}
  $tra_{last} = \frac{0.05}{0.18} \cdot hot_{last}$

□

... $tra_{last} = \frac{5}{18} \cdot hot_{last}$

⊩ $\dfrac{tra_{last}}{hot_{last} + tra_{last}}$

= {observation [2]}

$\dfrac{\frac{5}{18} \cdot hot_{last}}{hot_{last} + \frac{5}{18} \cdot hot_{last}}$

$=$ {cancel out hot_{last}}

$$\frac{\frac{5}{18}}{1+\frac{5}{18}}$$

$=$ {simplify}

$$\frac{5}{23}$$

$\approx$ {calculate an approximate value}

0.2173913

$\approx$ {round and write as a percentage}

21.7%

$\square$ 21.7%

The advantages and disadvantages of this format are quite obvious. The advantage is that it becomes easier to remember what the different quantities stand for, thus providing better guidance for intuition, and avoiding simple mistakes. The disadvantage is that the formulas become longer and somewhat less easy to read.

This style of naming variables is the norm in programs. Programs typically manipulate many different quantities, and giving one letter variable names to all these quantities becomes a problem. Therefore, one prefers to use short abbreviations as variable names. Specific areas of mathematics have their own naming conventions, which make it easier to remember what a quantity stands for. An example is mechanics, where s stands for distance, t for time, v for velocity and a for acceleration. Longer variable names is an alternative when solving problems in areas where there are no recognized naming conventions.

6.2 Is the Solution Correct

How do we know that our solution to the real-world problem is correct? And what does it mean to have a correct solution to a real-world problem? It turns out that there are two different notions of correctness that are relevant here.

- *Correctness of the mathematical solution*: Is the answer we obtain in the structured derivation the correct answer to the question given in the task? In other words: *have we solved the problem right?*

- *Correctness of the problem solution*: Is the solutions that we extracted from the answer the correct solution to original problem? In other words: *have we solved the right problem?*

These are two different things. Consider what can go wrong when we solve a word problem:

- The mathematical formulation of the informal problem may be wrong. We may have misunderstood what to do, or we have formulated an assumption incorrectly, omitted an assumption or added an assumption that is not included in the original problem. This means that we have solved the wrong problem. The informal problem formulation could also be ambiguous, so it may not even be possible to know exactly what the problem is. We can try to avoid errors in formulating the mathematical problem by carefully comparing the original problem text with the mathematical problem.

- The mathematical answer may be wrong. The problem has been formulated correctly, but we have made one or more errors in deriving the answer. In other words, we have a wrong solution to the mathematical problem. This is something that we can avoid by carefully going through the derivation itself, checking the justification of each step and verifying that the step is correct.

- The solution may have been interpreted wrongly. We have formulated the problem correctly, and the mathematical answer is also correct, but we have misinterpreted the answer. This means that we give an incorrect solution to the original task, even though everything was correct almost to the end.

- Finally, we may have evaluated the solution incorrectly. Maybe our solution is correct, but we do not realize it, or maybe it is incorrect, but we manage to convince ourselves that the solution is correct.

So there are a variety of things to take into account when giving a mathematical solution to a real world problem. And many of these errors can occur outside the realm of mathematics, in the formulation of the problem, the interpretation of the answer, or the plausibility check.

6.3 Assignments

1. The friends Amin, Anne, Ada and Arthur are eating pizza. Anne eats half a pizza and Amin eats two thirds of the amount that Anne eats. Ada is not as fond of the pizza, so she only eats half of what Amin ate. Arthur on the other hand is quite hungry, consuming three times the amount that Anne ate. How much pizza did the four friends devour in total?

2. An artist sketches a human body and contemplates the proportions of the body. She remembers from her time at the Academy of Arts that the head is $\frac{2}{15}$ of the entire body and the distance from the nose to the crown is $\frac{1}{2}$ of the height of the head (from the crown to the chin). Moreover the distance between the mouth and the nose should be $\frac{1}{2}$ of the distance between the chin and the nose. Help the artist calculate, what is the distance between the mouth and the crown as a fraction of the height of the body.

3. Anne in mixing some juice for herself. She should mix the juice at a ratio of 1 : 4, but she makes a minor mistake. She mixes 1.5 dl concentrate with water and gets 7 dl of mixed juice. At what proportions did Anna mix the juice?

4. You are determined to prove to the world that the number of times that a deck of cards can be ordered in is not really that large. Armed with the folly of youth you set forth going through the different ways that a deck of cards can be ordered in. Assume (in a manner patently hostile to reality) that you can arrange a pack of cards at a rate of one per second and that you never need to eat, sleep or drink. Would you have covered all of the permutations after a year?

5. A company that specializes in hot chili sauces wants to create a sauce with a specific strength, but the company only has two pepper mixtures. One mixture is 15% weaker than the desired strength, while the other mixture it 20% stronger than the desired strength. At what ratio should these mixtures be used to get the desired strength?

6. A shop owner raises the price of his doughnuts by 13%. This results in a 13% drop in sales. Did the increase in price pay off?

7. In 1883, the volcano Krakatoa had an eruption that released an amount of energy equivalent to 150 megatons of dynamite, i.e. $6.3 \cdot 10^{17}$ joules. In 1994, the collision between the comet Shoemaker-Levy and Jupiter released an amount of energy equivalent to 6 teratons of dynamite. How much energy was released during the collision of the Shoemaker-Levy?

CHAPTER 7

Structured Derivations

A task starts with a specific problem, and then continues to build a solution to this problem. The solution is carried out in some specific context, which lists the facts that we may use in our solution. However, there are often situations where we do not just have to formulate and solve a task, but where we must start with build the context for the task. A *structured derivation* describes both the context for one or more tasks, as well as the solutions to these tasks.

A structured derivation is essentially a *mathematical model* of some situation, together with an analysis of that model. The general way to build a mathematical model goes approximately as follows:

- We start from the specific situation that we want to analyze. This could be a real-world problem, or a purely theoretical problem in some domain of science. We identify the quantities that we need to measure, as well as those that we want to determine. We denote these quantities with constant names, and determine their value ranges.

- Next, we identify the constraints that these quantities satisfy and describe how they are related to each other.

- We then formulate the questions that we want to answer about the model. These are formulated as tasks to be solved.

- In order to answer the questions, we may need to first derive some basic facts about the situation, based on what has been defined so far.

- We may also need to define some new concepts, in order to make it easier to formulate constraints and questions about the model.

- We are then ready to determine the answers to the questions posed in the tasks.

- The answers to these tasks are then interpreted as statements/facts about the real-world situation that we are modeling.

7. Structured Derivations

7.1 Generalizing Tasks to Structured Derivations

A structured derivation is essentially a sequence of *derivation steps*, of the form

$$\textit{derivation step}$$
$$\vdots$$
$$\textit{derivation step}$$

where each derivation step is either

- an assumptions,
- an observations, or
- a tasks.

Assumptions, observations and tasks can thus be freely intermixed in a structured derivation.

A structured derivation allows us to work both on solving some specific tasks and on creating the proper context for these tasks. A structured derivation is the traditional way that a mathematician works on a problem. They first try to identify a specific problem to solve and formulate the problem in mathematical terms. Then they notice that more specific background assumptions are needed to formulate the problem, and that some new concepts have to be introduced by definitions. They then concentrate on solving the problem. Once they have solved the original problem, they may notice that there are other interesting questions that can also be solved in this same context. These may in turn require some additional assumptions and definitions, and so on.

The mathematical development unfolds as a novel, with a plot and some highlights. The difference, compared to a novel, is that each derivation step must be carefully checked for correctness, because a single incorrect observation, definition, or unjustified assumption can spoil the whole story. We also have to be careful not be caught in circular arguments (hence the linear format for the derivation).

A structured derivation gives us more freedom than a structured task:

- We are free to introduce definitions of concepts before we formulate assumptions or tasks that make use of these definitions.
- We can have any number of tasks based on the same set of assumptions, observations and definitions.
- We do not need to introduce all assumptions at once, we can introduce them one by one when they are needed.

7.1. Generalizing Tasks to Structured Derivations

Structured derivations are useful for problems with multiple questions. The next example shows a typical case of this: we first define a new concept, and then we ask a number of questions about this concept.

Example 35. The series $a_0, a_1, a_2, \ldots$ is defined by

$$a_n = \frac{n}{2n+1}$$

for $n = 0, 1, 2, 3, \ldots$. Show that (A) $0 < a_n < \frac{1}{2}$ when $n \geq 1$, that (B) $a_{n+1} > a_n$ when $n \geq 0$ and (C) calculate $\lim_{n \to \infty} a_n$.

We solve this task with a general structured derivation. Note that instead of bullets, we indicate the tasks with capital letters, A, B, and C.

+ $a : \mathbb{N} \to \mathbb{R}$ {the function a describes a series, where we denote $a_i = a(i)$, $i = 0, 1, 2, \ldots$. The series is well defined, since $2n + 1 > 0$ when $n = 0, 1, 2, \ldots$ }

      $a_n = \dfrac{n}{2n+1}$ when $n = 0, 1, 2, 3, \ldots$

A.   Show that $0 < a_n < \dfrac{1}{2}$, when

-     $n : \mathbb{N}, n \geq 1$

⊩ $0 < a_n < \dfrac{1}{2}$

≡   {use the definition of a_n}

      $0 < \dfrac{n}{2n+1} < \dfrac{1}{2}$

≡   {multiply both sides by $2n+1$, write as a conjunction}

      $0 < n \land n < \dfrac{2n+1}{2}$

≡   {simplify}

      $0 < n \land 2n < 2n+1$

≡   {$n \geq 1$ by the assumption, so the first proposition is true; the second proposition is always true}

      true

□

B.   Show that $a_{n+1} > a_n$, when

83

7. STRUCTURED DERIVATIONS

-     $n : \mathbb{N}$

⊩ $a_{n+1} > a_n$

≡   {use the definition of a_n}

$$\frac{n+1}{2(n+1)+1} > \frac{n}{2n+1}$$

≡   {simplify}

$$\frac{n+1}{2n+3} > \frac{n}{2n+1}$$

≡   {multiply by $(2n+3)(2n+1)$, which, by the assumption, is positive}

$$(2n+1)(n+1) > (2n+3)n$$

≡   {simplify}

$$2n^2 + 3n + 1 > 2n^2 + 3n$$

≡   {subtract $2n^2 + 3n$ from both sides}

$$1 > 0$$

≡   {arithmetics}

$$true$$

□

C.   Calculate $\lim_{n \to \infty} a_n$

⊩ $\lim_{n \to \infty} a_n$

=   {the definition}

$$\lim_{n \to \infty} \frac{n}{2n+1}$$

=   {reduce by n }

$$\lim_{n \to \infty} \frac{\frac{n}{n}}{\frac{2n}{n} + \frac{1}{n}}$$

=   {simplify}

$$\lim_{n \to \infty} \frac{1}{2 + \frac{1}{n}}$$

= $\{\frac{1}{n} \to 0$ when $n \to \infty\}$

$$\frac{1}{2}$$

☐ $\lim_{n\to\infty} a_n = \dfrac{1}{2}$ ∎

Structured derivations generalize all the previously defined constructs. A structured task is, e.g., a special case of a structured derivation, where there is only one derivation step, a task. Similarly, a simple fact, a definition, or a sequence of facts and definitions, are also special cases of a structured derivations.

We may look at a structured derivation as a *model*, a *theory*, an *example*, or something similar. We would give a name to the derivation, e.g., with the following syntax:

- *model name*

  derivation_step

  $\vdots$

  derivation_step

  ☐

Typically, we could have a theory like *Group theory*, or *Lattice theory*, or a model like *Company inventory*, and so on. This would introduce a range of new issues that would need to be dealt with: how is this theory related to other theories, does it make use of concepts introduced in other theories, is it an extension of some other theory, what are the main properties of theories, how can we build and analyze theories, etc. This goes beyond the standard content of high school mathematics, so we will not go more deeply into this issue here. We will, however, consider questions of this kind in the sequel to the present book, where we take a more logic based approach to structured derivations.

7.2 Modeling with Structured Derivations

We showed earlier how to formulate and solve a word problem as a mathematical task. We will here show how to formulate and solve a word problem as structured derivation. This means that we first construct a mathematical model for the word problem, before formulating the question we want to answer. We use a structured derivation for the example problem below, because we need some preliminary definitions before formulating the problem that we want to solve. These definitions could also be given outside the derivation, as background information, but we include them here in the derivation, to show how the modeling process can be used also for simple examples.

Example 36. (FNME, Autumn 2002) Since the year 1960 the travel time of the fastest train connection between Helsinki and Lappeenranta has decreased by 37%.

7. STRUCTURED DERIVATIONS

Calculate by how many percent the average speed has increased. Assume that the length of the railroad has not changed.

Analyzing the problem statement, we see that we will need notations for the length of the railroad, for the time the trip used to take, and for the time it now takes, in order to express the assumptions in the problem:

- $s : \mathbb{R}$ — the length of the track
- $t : \mathbb{R}$ — the original travel time
- $t' : \mathbb{R}$ — the current travel time

There is no need to introduce a symbol for the current length of the track, since we may assume that it is unchanged.

We can then formulate the following assumption:

(a) t' is 37% less than t — the current travel time is 37 % less than the original travel time

All variables must be positive real numbers, for the task to be meaningful. We can therefore add assumption (b).

(b) $t > 0$, $t' > 0$ and $s > 0$ — follows from the formulation of the problem

In order to formulate the question in the task, we also need to introduce symbols for the original speed (v), the current speed (v'), and the increase in speed (p). We must show that this new notation is well-defined.

[1] $v : \mathbb{R}$ — the original speed

{definition of speed, can be used, since $t > 0$ according to (b)}

$$v = \frac{s}{t}$$

[2] $v' : \mathbb{R}$ — the current speed

{definition of speed, can be used, since $t' > 0$ according to (b)}

$$v' = \frac{s}{t'}$$

[3] $p : \mathbb{R}$ — increase in speed

{definition of speed increase, can be used since $s > 0$, from which it follows that $v > 0$}

$$p = \frac{v' - v}{v}$$

7.2. Modeling with Structured Derivations

We can now write down what we are supposed to do, as a task.

- Calculate p — the increase in the speed of the trip between Helsinki and Lappeenranta

We begin solving this by writing assumption (a) more precisely:

[4] {calculate the current travel time, based on (a)}

- $t - t' = 0.37 \cdot t$
- ≡ {subtract t from both sids}

  $-t' = 0.37 \cdot t - t$
- ≡ {simplify}

  $-t' = -0.63 \cdot t$
- ≡ {divide by -1}

  $t' = 0.63 \cdot t$

□

… $t' = 0.63 \cdot t$

The formulation of the problem is now ready, and we can start to work on the solution. We get the following calculation:

⊩ p

=   {observation [3]}

$$\frac{v' - v}{v}$$

=   {observation [1] and [2]}

$$\frac{\frac{s}{t'} - \frac{s}{t}}{\frac{s}{t}}$$

=   {simplify}

$$\frac{\frac{s}{t'}}{\frac{s}{t}} - 1$$

=   {simplify the fractions}

$$\frac{s \cdot t}{s \cdot t'} - 1$$

=   {simplify}

7. STRUCTURED DERIVATIONS

$$\frac{t}{t'} - 1$$

$=$ {$t' = 0.63 \cdot t$ according to observation [4], cancel out t}

$$\frac{1}{0.63} - 1$$

$\approx$ {calculate an approximate value of the expression}

0.59

$=$ {write as a percentage}

59%

□ $\quad p \approx 59\%$ — the increase in speed

Thus, the answer is that the speed for the fastest connection between Helsinki and Lappeenranta has increased with 59 % since the 1960.

Remark. The solutions to the modeling problems presented above are quite long, considering the rather simple calculations involved. A trained person can get the answers quite a lot faster and with less effort, by just writing down the relevant equations and solving them directly. The purpose of the two examples above is to show how to derive a solution where every step is carefully justified. At the same time, this provides a checklist of all the information that actually needs to go into the problem formulation and the solution. In practice, much of this information is left implicit. However, if you want to be very careful and certain that the calculation is correct, or if you are teaching problem solving skills to students with little prior experience in this, then it might be a good idea to spell out all steps explicitly. First teach the students how to do it properly, before teaching them the shortcuts.

The following sections gives further and more advanced examples of how to use structured derivations in modeling.

7.3 Example from Geometry

Example 37. (FNME, Autumn 2002). One of the angles in a triangle is α, and its opposite side has the length 5; another angle is 2α and its opposite side has the length 8. Calculate the exact length of the third side of the triangle, and calculate α with accuracy within a tenth of a degree.

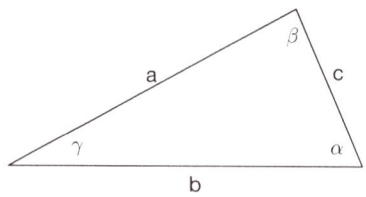

7.3. Example from Geometry

Let us start by listing the facts that are given in the assignment, giving names to the important entities at the same time:

(a) The geometric figure is a triangle, with sides a, b and c, and opposing angles α, β and γ

(b) $a = 5$

(c) $b = 8$

(d) $\beta = 2\alpha$

Let us check that we have all assumptions and assignments written down correctly. For this, we write down the informal problem statement once again, and mark the text fragments with the corresponding entities in the derivation. We mark the assumptions blue and the tasks magenta.

> One of the angles in a triangle is α (assumption a), and its opposite side has the length 5 (assumption b); another angle is 2α (assumption d) and its opposite side has the length 8 (assumption c). Calculate the exact length of the third side of the triangle (task B) , and calculate α with accuracy within a tenth of a degree (task A).

We can see that all assumptions from the informal problem statement have been taken into account in the derivation, and that there are no extra entities (assumptions or tasks) in the derivation. We have also marked the tasks that we need to solve in the problem statement.

We will first calculate the angle α.

A. Calculate the angle α

⊩ {Two of the the angles and the lengths of two of the sides are known in the triangle, so we can use the law of sines, $\dfrac{a}{\sin(\alpha)} = \dfrac{b}{\sin(\beta)} = \dfrac{c}{\sin(\gamma)}$ and fill in the values from the assumptions}

$$\dfrac{5}{\sin(\alpha)} = \dfrac{8}{\sin(2\alpha)}$$

≡ {multiply both sides by $\sin(\alpha)$ and $\sin(2\alpha)$; the sufficient restriction $0° < \alpha, 2\alpha < 180°$ follows from (a) which says that the figure is a triangle}

$$5\sin(2\alpha) = 8\sin(\alpha)$$

≡ {$\sin(2\alpha) = 2\sin(\alpha)\cos(\alpha)$}

$$5 \cdot 2\sin(\alpha)\cos(\alpha) = 8\sin(\alpha)$$

≡ {divide by $\sin(\alpha)$; this is allowed because $\sin(\alpha) \neq 0$ ($\alpha \neq 0°$ and $\alpha \neq 180°$ in a triangle)}

7. Structured Derivations

$$10 \cos \alpha = 8$$

≡ {divide both sides by 10 and simplify}

$$\cos(\alpha) = \frac{4}{5}$$

□ Angle α is such that $\cos(\alpha) = \frac{4}{5}$

[1] {From the solution to task A, calculating the approximate value for α and rounding it off in accordance with the condition}

$$\alpha \approx 36.9°$$

Having calculated the angle α, our next task is to calculate the length of the third side in the triangle.

B. Calculate the length of c

⊢ {Two sides and one angle are known in a triangle, so the law of cosines $a^2 = b^2 + c^2 - 2bc \cdot \cos \alpha$ can be used to find the third side}

$$5^2 = 8^2 + c^2 - 2 \cdot 8 \cdot c \cdot \cos(\alpha)$$

≡ {task A}

$$5^2 = 8^2 + c^2 - 2 \cdot 8 \cdot c \cdot \frac{4}{5}$$

≡ {write it in the form $ax^2 + bx + c = 0$}

$$c^2 - \frac{64}{5}c + 39 = 0$$

≡ {solve the equation with the quadratic formula}

$$c = \frac{-(-\frac{64}{5}) \pm \sqrt{(-\frac{64}{5})^2 - 4 \cdot 1 \cdot 39}}{2 \cdot 1}$$

≡ {simplify}

$$c = \frac{64}{10} \pm \frac{\sqrt{\frac{196}{25}}}{2}$$

≡ $\{\sqrt{\frac{a}{b}} = \frac{\sqrt{a}}{\sqrt{b}}\}$

$$c = \frac{64}{10} \pm \frac{\left(\frac{\sqrt{196}}{\sqrt{25}}\right)}{2}$$

≡ {compute the square roots and simplify}

$$c = \frac{64}{10} \pm \frac{14}{10}$$

≡ {write as disjunction}

$c = 7.8 \;\vee\; c = 5$

≡ {the answer $c = 5$ is false, as the triangle would then be an isosceles with the angles α, α, and 2α, but according to [1], $4\alpha \approx 147.6°$ and $147.6 \neq 180°$. Therefore the figure would not be a triangle, so $c = 5 \equiv false$}

$c = 7.8 \;\vee\; false$

≡ {$p \vee false \equiv p$}

$c = 7.8$

☐ Third side $c = 7.8$ ∎

7.4 Example from Probability Theory

Example 38. (FNME, Autumn 2002). Lena and Sarah toss a coin to decide which one of them will get to ride a horse first. Lena tosses the coin first and is allowed to ride first if she gets a head. If she gets a tail, Sarah will toss the coin and will ride first if she gets a head. If Sarah also gets a tail, the turn to toss the coin goes to Lena again. They continue in this manner until one of them gets a head. What is the probability the Lena is allowed to ride first? What is the probability that Sarah is allowed to ride first?

Let us again start with what we know about the problem.

(a) The probability of the event "head" is $\frac{1}{2}$

(b) The probability of the event "tail" is $\frac{1}{2}$

(c) A "head" lets one ride first, and the coin is tossed until a "head" is acquired

(d) The girls takes turns in tossing the coin

(e) Lena gets the first throw

We then determine the probabilities involving Lena.

[1] $q : [0, 1]$ {Determine the probability q that a person lands a head/tail after she has landed a tail. This event can only take place if the second person has landed a tail (probability $\frac{1}{2}$), thus giving the first person a chance to throw again (probability $\frac{1}{2}$ regardless of whether she lands a head or a tail). Hence, $q = \frac{1}{2} \cdot \frac{1}{2} = \frac{1}{4}$.}

7. STRUCTURED DERIVATIONS

$q = \frac{1}{4}$

[2] {The total probability that Lena is allowed to ride first is given by the expression $\frac{1}{2} + \frac{1}{2} \cdot q + \frac{1}{2} \cdot q^2 + \ldots + \frac{1}{2} \cdot q^n + \ldots$, $n \in \mathbb{N}$, (the probability that she gets to ride on the first turn is $\frac{1}{2}$, $\frac{1}{2}q$ on the second turn and so forth)}

$$P(\text{"Lena rides first"}) = \frac{1}{2} + \frac{1}{2} \cdot q + \frac{1}{2} \cdot q^2 + \ldots + \frac{1}{2} \cdot q^n + \ldots, n \in \mathbb{N}$$

We now consider the situation from Lena's point of view.

A. Calculate the probability that Lena is allowed to ride first

⊢ $P(\text{"Lena rides first"})$

= {observation [2]}

$\frac{1}{2} + \frac{1}{2} \cdot q + \frac{1}{2} \cdot q^2 + \ldots + \frac{1}{2} \cdot q^n + \ldots$

= {This series is a infinite geometric series. Since $q = \frac{1}{4} < 1$ according to [1], the value of the series is given by $\frac{a}{1-q}$ when $|q| < 1$. Here the first term a is $\frac{1}{2}$}

$\frac{\frac{1}{2}}{1 - \frac{1}{4}}$

= {calculate}

$\frac{2}{3}$

□ $P(\text{"Lena rides first"}) = \frac{2}{3}$

From this we can immediately infer the probability that Sarah rides first.

[3] {Sarah rides with probability $1 - P(\text{"Lena rides first"})$}

$$P(\text{"Sarah rides first"}) = \frac{1}{3}$$

The situation involves an unbounded number of throws, so we might be a little bit uncertain about the last observation. We therefore check the answer for Sarah by doing a similar calculation that we did above for Lena, but now from Sarah's point of view.

[5] {Lena gets a head with her first toss with the probability $\frac{1}{2}$. If she lands a tail instead, Sarah will have the probability $\frac{1}{2}$ to land a head.}

Sarah is allowed to ride with her first toss with probability $\frac{1}{4}$.

[6] {The total probability that Sarah is allowed to ride first is given by the expression $\frac{1}{4} + \frac{1}{4} \cdot q + \frac{1}{4} \cdot q^2 + ... + \frac{1}{4} \cdot q^n + ..., n \in \mathbb{N}.$}

$P(\text{"Sarah rides first"}) = \frac{1}{4} + \frac{1}{4} \cdot q + \frac{1}{4} \cdot q^2 + ... + \frac{1}{4} \cdot q^n + ..., n \in \mathbb{N}.$

B. Calculate the probability that Sarah is allowed ride first.

⊩ $P(\text{"Sarah rides first"})$

=   {observation [6]}

$\frac{1}{4} + \frac{1}{4} \cdot q + \frac{1}{4} \cdot q^2 + ... + \frac{1}{4} \cdot q^n + ...$

=   {the series above is a infinite geometric series with value $\frac{a}{1-q}$ when $|q| < 1$. The first term a is given by $\frac{1}{4}$}

$\frac{\frac{1}{4}}{1 - \frac{1}{4}}$

=   {calculate}

$\frac{1}{3}$

☐ $P(\text{"Sarah rides first"}) = \frac{1}{3}$

This shows that the original answers were correct: Lena rides first with probability $\frac{2}{3}$ and Sarah rides first with probability $\frac{1}{3}$. ∎

7.5 Example from Mechanics

Example 39. Sergeant Riley shoots a cannon ball straight upwards with a canon placed on the ground. The initial velocity of the cannon ball is 80 m/s, and air friction is assumed to be negligible. On what height above ground is the cannonball when 6.0 seconds has passed. Is the cannon ball still going upwards at this point of time?

Let us start by considering what we know.

-    $y : \mathbb{R}^+ \to \mathbb{R}$ — the height of the ball, as a function of time

7. STRUCTURED DERIVATIONS

- $y_0 : \mathbb{R}$ — initial height of the ball
- $v_0 : \mathbb{R}$ — initial velocity
- $a : \mathbb{R}$ — uniform acceleration

(a) $v_0 = 80\,\text{m/s}$ — the initial velocity of the cannon ball

(b) 6.0 seconds have passed

(c) The cannon ball is shot from ground level

(d) Air resistance is negligible

We then make some initial observations.

[1] {Law of mechanics, the height of ball y as a function of time t}

$y(t) = y_0 + v_0 t + \tfrac{1}{2} a t^2$, for $t \geq 0$

[2] {from (c), initial height y_0 is 0 }

$y_0 = 0$

[3] {the uniform acceleration due to Earths gravitation}

$a = g = -9.81\,\text{m/s}^2$

A. Calculate height of ball when 6.0 seconds have passed.

⊩ [1]

⇒ {Compute height for time $t = 6.0$ s}

$y(6) = y_0 + v_0 \cdot 6.0\,\text{s} + \tfrac{1}{2} a \cdot (6.0\,\text{s})^2$,

⇒ {Insert initial velocity v_0 from (a), initial height y_0 from [2] and acceleration a from [3]}

$y(6) = 0 + 80\,\text{m/s} \cdot 6.0s - \tfrac{1}{2} \cdot (-9.81\,\text{m/s}^2) \cdot (6.0\,\text{s})^2$

≡ {Calculate}

$y(6) = 303.42\,\text{m}$

□ The height of the ball is 303.42 m after 6.0 seconds

Next we determine whether the ball is still on its way up after 6.0 seconds.

B. Is the ball still rising after 6.0 seconds?

⊩ ball is still rising at time 6.0

≡ {the ball is still rising when the velocity is positive}

velocity is positive at time 6.0

$\equiv$ {velocity is time derivative of distance}

- $\frac{d}{dt}y(t)$
= {[1]}
  $\frac{d}{dt}(y_0 + v_0 t + \frac{1}{2}at^2)$
= {calculate derivative}
  $v_0 + at$

□

... $v_0 + a \cdot 6.0\,\text{s} > 0$

$\equiv$ {insert values from (a) and [3]}

$80\,\text{m/s} + (-9.81\,\text{m/s}^2) \cdot 6.0\,\text{s} > 0$

$\equiv$ {calculate}

$21.14\,\text{m/s} > 0$

$\equiv$ {true fact}

$true$

□ Yes, the ball is still rising at time 6.0 seconds. ■

7.6 Example from Nuclear Physics

Example 40. Calculate the missing mass in the fusion reaction between deuterium and tritium, $^2_1H + ^3_1H \rightarrow ^4_2He + ^1_0n$. Determine whether energy is consumed or released in this reaction. Give the answer with the precision of four decimals. The interior of a certain star converts every minute at least 45 billion tons of hydrogen to helium (compare to the 36 billion tons converted by our own sun). Assume that all this energy is due to the reaction above. Calculate the power of the star.

We start by listing the facts that we will be using in our calculations.

(a) We study the reaction $^2_1H + ^3_1H \rightarrow ^4_2He + ^1_0n$

[1] {The mass of the atom nucleus is the mass of the atom/isotope minus the mass of the electrons, where a is the number of electrons in the isotope}

$m(nucleus) = m(isotope) - a \cdot m(e)$

A. Calculate the missing mass Δm.

⊩ Δm

7. Structured Derivations

$=$	{The missing mass Δm is given by the difference between the mass of the initial reactants and the mass of the product of the reaction. Use [1] to calculate the mass of each nucleus}

$$m(^2_1H) - m(e) + m(^3_1H) - m(e) - (m(^4_2He) - 2m(e) + m(^1_0n))$$

$=$	{The masses of the electrons cancel each other}

$$m(^2_1H) + m(^3_1H) - (m(^4_2He) + m(^1_0n))$$

$=$	{Insert the values for the isotope masses: $m(^2_1H) = 2.0141018\,\text{u}$, $m(^3_1H) = 3.0160493\,\text{u}$, $m(^4_2He) = 4.0026033\,\text{u}$ and $m(^1_0n) = 1.0086650\,\text{u}$. Calculate the result}

0.0188828 u

☐ $\Delta m = 0.0188828\,\text{u}$

B. Calculate the energy E that is released in the reaction (a)

⊢ E

$=$ {The reaction energy is the missing mass converted into energy}

$\Delta m \cdot c^2$

$=$ {A}

$0.0188828\,\text{u} \cdot c^2$

$=$ {$1\text{u} = 1.6605402 \cdot 10^{-27}\,\text{kg}$}

$0.0188828 \cdot 1.6605402 \cdot 10^{-27}\,\text{kg} \cdot c^2$

$=$ {$c = 299792458\,\text{m/s}$}

$0.0188828 \cdot 1.6605402 \cdot 10^{-27}\,\text{kg} \cdot (299792458\,\text{m/s})^2$

$=$ {Calculate}

$2.81810514617 \cdot 10^{-12}\,\text{J}$

☐ $E = 2.81810514617 \cdot 10^{-12}\,\text{J}$

C. Calculate E in electron volts, with four decimal precision

⊢ E

$=$ {convert to electron volt}

17.5892212017 MeV

$\approx$ {Round off to two decimals}

17.59 MeV

7.6. Example from Nuclear Physics

- □ $E = 17.59\,\text{MeV}$

(b) The star converts 45 billion tons of hydrogen to helium each minute

(c) The reaction (a) is the only one going on in the sun

[2] {The mass of the hydrogen nuclei that participate in the reaction is their combined mass}

-      •   mass of hydrogen nuclei in the reaction
- =   {the hydrogen nuclei are ^2_1H and ^3_1H, according to (a)}

  $m(^2_1H) + m(^3_1H)$
- =   {insert values for the masses}

  $2.0141018\,\text{u} + 3.0160493\,\text{u}$
- =   {add and convert to kilogram, $1\,\text{u} = 1.6605402 \cdot 10^{-27}\,\text{kg}$}

  $8.3527681 \cdot 10^{-27}\,\text{kg}$
- □

... The combined mass of the hydrogen nuclei is $8.3527681 \cdot 10^{-27}\,\text{kg}$

[3] $n : \mathbb{R}$ {The number of reactions n taking place each minute is the total mass of hydrogen being converted divided by the the mass needed for one reaction}

$n = \frac{45 \cdot 10^{12}\,\text{kg}}{8.3527681 \cdot 10^{-27}\,\text{kg}}$

D. Calculate the power P of the star

⊩ P

=   {The power is work divided by time}

     W/t

=   {Work is here total amount of energy released in one minute}

     nE/t

=   {[3]}

     $\frac{45 \cdot 10^{12}\,\text{kg}}{8.3527681 \cdot 10^{-27}\,\text{kg}} \cdot E/t$

=   {E is given by (B) and $t = 60\,\text{s}$}

     $\frac{45 \cdot 10^{12}\,\text{kg}}{8.3527681 \cdot 10^{-27}\,\text{kg}} \cdot 2.81810514617 \cdot 10^{-12}\,\text{J} / 60\,\text{s}$

=   {Calculate}

     $2.53039331498 \cdot 10^{26}\,\text{W}$

≈   {Approximate}

$2.5 \cdot 10^{26}$ W

☐ The power of the sun is approximately $2.5 \cdot 10^{26}$ W (in reality it would be higher due to the other reactions taking place).

There are a number of calculation steps above, so we need to summarize the results and check that we are actually answering the original questions. Based on these calculations, we get the following answers:

1. The missing mass in the reaction is $\Delta m = 0.0188828\,\text{u}$ (A)
2. Energy is released in the reaction, the released energy is $E = 17.59\,\text{MeV}$ (C)
3. The power of the star is $2.5 \cdot 10^{26}$ W (D)

∎

7.7 Assignments

1. Solve the equation $|x^n| = x^{n+1}$, where n is a positive integer.

2. Determine for which values of a the expression $\ln\left((x^2 + x)\left(\frac{x+1}{x-1}\right)\right)$ is defined.

3. A space age ruler, who has way too much money, time and cubist passions, wants the Universe to contain at least one cubic object. For this reason, he has the trans-Neptunian dwarf planet Sedna transformed into a cube. a) Calculate the side length of the cube, when Sedna's radius is 995 km and the ruler has access to technology that is advanced enough to use the entire mass of Sedna to create the cube. b) What if the ruler had preferred more traditional methods and transformed the spherical Sedna into a cube by cutting off excess matter. Calculate the volume of Cube-Sedna and the percentage of the original planet that was wasted in the transformation. You may assume that Sedna is spherical and that its mass is uniformly distributed.

4. The barrel of an old cannon is cylindrical. The volume of the cannonballs they used is $8.5\,\text{dm}^3$ and eight of them fit into the barrel so that the last one precisely reaches the muzzle of the barrel. Patrick the Pirate gets overexcited when he loads the cannon with gunpowder. The result is that only a single cannonball barely fits inside the muzzle. a) Calculate the volume of the barrel. b) How much gunpowder did Patrick put into the cannon, when none of it is in front of the cannonball and there is only one cannonball in the barrel?

5. Four letters are randomly picked out of the eleven-letter word UNFORTU-NATE. Determine the probability that a) only one of the letters is a consonant, b) only one of the letters is a vowel, and c) you can spell TUNA with the letters that are picked out.

6. Let the function $f : \mathbb{R} \to \mathbb{R}$ be $f(x) = x^4 + 5x + 2$. a) Differentiate $f(x)$. b) Determine $f'(2)$. c) Determine the smallest value of $f(x)$.

7.7. Assignments

7. May is designing a sturdy table inspired by mathematical curves. She uses the solid of revolution generated by rotating the curve $y = 0.2x^2 - 3x + 15$ around the x-axis on the interval $[1, 20]$. Determine a) the volume of the of the solid of revolution (in volume units), b) how much wood it takes to create the table, if it is 95 cm high, c) how much does the table weight if it is made out of oak with a density of 700 kg/m³, and d) how much varnish will it take to coat every surface of the table when you use around 0.12 liters of varnish to cover a square meter.

CHAPTER 8

Checking Correctness

How do we know that a structured derivation is correct? We have previously defined what it means for a structured calculation to be correct, as well as what it means for a observation to be correct, and what it means for an answer to be correct in a simple task. We have not, however, yet defined correctness for a arbitrary structured task, with possible nested tasks, nor for structured derivations in general. This is our task in this chapter.

8.1 Correctness of Tasks

Let us first consider the correctness of a structured task. Assume that the task is of the form

- *question*
- Φ
- ⋮ (observations)
- ⊩ *justification*
- ⋮ (calculation)
- □ *answer*

Definition 7. The task above is correct in the external context Φ_0, if

(a) the observations are correct in the context of Φ_0 and Φ,

8. CHECKING CORRECTNESS

(b) the calculation steps are correct in the context of Φ_0, Φ, and the observations, and

(b) *justification* proves that the answer is correct in the context of Φ_0, Φ, the observations, and the calculation steps.

■

Questions and answers in tasks are intended to focus the attention on what we are supposed to do. Once we have found the answer to the question, proving that the answer is correct can also be expressed as proving the correctness of an equivalent proof task. Below, we show a some-task on the left and the corresponding proof task on the right. The proof obligations are the same in these two tasks.

- • $?\, x : A : Q(x)$
- – Φ
- ⋮   (observations)
- ⊩   *justification*
- ⋮   (calculation)
- □ $x = t$

- • $t \in A \wedge Q(t)$
- – Φ
- ⋮   (observations)
- ⊩   *justification*
- ⋮   (calculation)
- □

Similarly, we can also rewrite an all-task as an equivalent proof task. Below is an all-task on the left and the corresponding proof task on the right.

- • $!\, x : A : Q(x)$
- – Φ
- ⋮   (observations)
- ⊩   *justification*
- ⋮   (calculation)
- □ $R(x)$

- • $R(x) \equiv Q(x)$
- – Φ
- – $x \in A$
- ⋮   (observations)
- ⊩   *justification*
- ⋮   (calculation)
- □

8.1. Correctness of Tasks

Note that we have added the assumption $x \in A$ in the proof task, as we want to prove that $R(x) \equiv Q(x)$ for every $x \in A$. The original task and the corresponding proof task are equivalent, in the sense that they give rise to the same proof obligations.

This means that the question of whether an all- or some-task is correct or not can be reduced to the simpler question of whether the corresponding proof task is correct or not. This gives us the following definition.

Definition 8. A structured task is correct in the external context Φ_0, if the corresponding proof task is correct in this same context.

Finally, we also need to be more specific about what we mean when we say that a justification proves some property Q in a given context Φ. For a simple justification, with an explanation in curly brackets and no nested tasks, this means that the explanation is sufficient to justify why property Q follows from the assumptions Φ. This is a basic mathematical fact of the form $\Phi \vdash Q$ by $\{explanation\}$. We assume that the correctness of this can be checked directly.

The situation is more complicated when we have a justification with nested tasks. In this case, the explanation rests on the assumption that the nested tasks are correct, so we need to check these also. The use of nested tasks requires us to be explicit about the context in which we prove something, because the context for a nested task may be different from the context of the enclosing task.

Assume that *justification* has the following form:

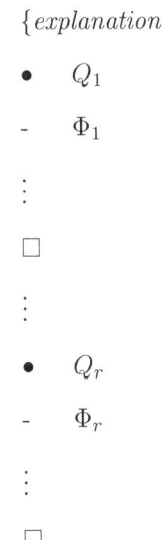

We assume here that the nested tasks are all proof tasks, and that the context of the justification is Φ. As we showed above, any task can be written as an equivalent

8. CHECKING CORRECTNESS

proof task. The first nested task above shows that Q_1 is true in the context Φ and Φ_1, the second that Q_2 is true in the context Φ and Φ_2, ..., and the last shows that Q_r is true in the context Φ and Φ_r.

Definition 9. Assume that *justification* has the form above. Then *justification* proves the property Q in the context Φ (i.e., $\Phi \vdash Q$ by *justification*), if

(a) each nested task in the justification is correct in the context Φ, and

(b) *explanation* shows that Q is true in the context Φ extended with the properties proved in the nested tasks, $(\Phi \wedge \Phi_1 \Rightarrow Q_1), \ldots, (\Phi \wedge \Phi_r \Rightarrow Q_r)$.[1]

∎

The recursive nature of structured tasks means that the definition of correctness of a task is reduced to the correctness of the justifications in the task. Correctness of these are again reduced to the correctness of their nested tasks, and so on. As before, the recursion ends with justifications that do not contain nested tasks.

Example 41. Consider the structured task of Example 28. Assume that the external context Φ is here the theory of natural numbers and arithmetic. The original task is the text written in black below. The text written in red shows, for each justification, what exactly needs to be true. The red text thus shows the basic mathematical facts that this proof task is based on.

- Show that $k^2 + k$ is even, when

(a) k is a natural number

⊩   {Φ, (a),

     (k is an even number $\Rightarrow k^2 + k$ is even),

     (k is an odd number $\Rightarrow k^2 + k$ is even)

     $\vdash k^2 + k$ is even {case analysis}}

-    Show that $k^2 + k$ is even, when

(b) k is an even number

⊩   {Φ, (a), (b), calculation steps $\vdash k^2 + k$ is even {transitivity}}

     $k^2 + k$ is even

≡   {Φ, (a), (b) $\vdash k^2 + k$ is even $\equiv k(k+1)$ is even {write as product}}

     $k(k+1)$ is even

---

[1] In other words, (b) says that we need to prove that
$$\Phi, (\Phi \wedge \Phi_1 \Rightarrow Q_1), \ldots, (\Phi \wedge \Phi_r \Rightarrow Q_r) \vdash Q$$

⇐ $\{\Phi, (a), (b) \vdash k(k+1) \text{ is even} \Leftarrow k \text{ is even } \{\text{a product is even if one of the factors is even}\}\}$

k is even

≡ $\{\Phi, (a), (b) \vdash k \text{ is odd} \equiv true \; \{\text{assumption}\}\}$

$true$

□

- Show that $k^2 + k$ is even, when
(c) k is an odd number

⊩ $\{\Phi, (a), (c), \text{calculation steps} \vdash k^2 + k \text{ is even } \{\text{transitivity}\}\}$

$k^2 + k$ is even

≡ $\{\Phi, (a), (c) \vdash k^2 + k \text{ is even} \equiv k(k+1) \text{ is even } \{\text{write as product}\}\}$

$k(k+1)$ is even

⇐ $\{\Phi, (a), (c) \vdash k(k+1) \text{ is even} \Leftarrow k+1 \text{ is even } \{\text{a product is even if one of the factors is even}\}\}$

$k+1$ is even

≡ $\{\Phi, (a), (c) \vdash k+1 \text{ is even} \equiv k \text{ is odd } \{\text{number theory}\}\}$

k is odd

≡ $\{\Phi, (a), (c) \vdash k \text{ is odd} \equiv true \; \{\text{assumption}\}\}$

$true$

□

□

The example shows how the question of whether the task is correct is reduced to the correctness of the basic mathematical facts used in the task (written in red). If all these facts are correct, then the proof task is also correct, and the proposition has been proved, i.e., we have proved that $k^2 + k$ is even when k is a natural number. If even one of these basic facts would turn out to be false, then we don't have a proof of the proposition.

8.2 Correctness of Structured Derivations

We have shown earlier that a structured task can be expressed as an equivalent proof task. A proof task of the form on the left below can again be expressed as an equivalent fact, shown below on the right:

8. CHECKING CORRECTNESS

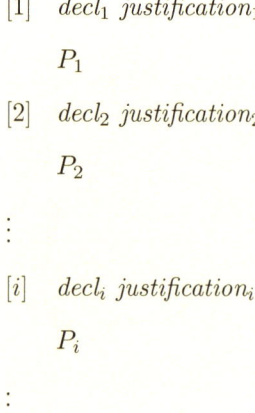

$$\ldots \wedge \Phi \Rightarrow Q$$

Here $\wedge \Phi$ stands for the conjunction of all assumptions in Φ. This step is based on the standard method of proving an implication $A \Rightarrow B$, by proving B under assumptions A.

This shows that we can replace each task in a structured derivation with a corresponding equivalent fact. Hence, we need only consider structured derivations with assumptions, facts and definitions.

Let us write a structured derivation of this form as

[1] $decl_1$ $justification_1$

P_1

[2] $decl_2$ $justification_2$

P_2

$\vdots$

[i] $decl_i$ $justification_i$

P_i

$\vdots$

Here

- $decl_i$ and $justification_i$ are both empty (missing) if $[i]$ is an assumption,
- $decl_i$ is empty if $[i]$ is a fact, and

- neither $decl_i$ nor $justification_i$ is empty if $[i]$ is a definition.

Definition 10. We say that step $[i]$ in the above derivation is *correct* in the external context Φ, if either

(a) $[i]$ is an assumption, or

(b) $[i]$ is a fact and $justification_i$ proves P_i in the context $\Phi, P_1, \ldots, P_{i-1}$, or

(c) $[i]$ is a definition where $decl_i$ is $x_i : T_i$, and $justification_i$ proves that there exist a value $x_i \in T_i$ that satisfies the condition P_i, in the context $\Phi, P_1, \ldots, P_{i-1}$.

We say that the structured derivation above is *correct*, if each derivation step is correct.

∎

The definitions above now show how to check that a structured derivation is correct.

8.3 Checklists for Structured Derivations

We will summarize the rules for checking that a structured derivation is correct in three checklists: checking the correctness of a structured task, checking the correctness of a justification with nested tasks, and checking the correctness of a structured derivation. These checklists just repeat the definitions that we have given earlier, but may provide an easier overview of what exactly we have to check at each derivation step. We check that a structured derivation is correct by reducing it to a collection of basic mathematical facts, and checking each basic fact separately.

Checklist for a task We assume that the task is carried out in an external context Φ. On the left hand side, we have the general syntax of a task. We assume for simplicity that all facts are listed before the definitions, although in general these may come in arbitrary order. Here $A_1, \ldots, A_m$ are assumptions, $P_1, \ldots, P_n$ are facts, $Q_1, \ldots, Q_h$ are definition constraints, and $t_0, t_2, \ldots, t_k$ are expressions. The existentially quantified property $(\exists y_1 : T_1 : Q_1)$ stands for "there exists a value y_1 in T_1 such that Q_1 is true for this value".

On the right hand side, we have the mathematical fact that needs to be proved in order for this step to be correct, in the form $\Phi \vdash P$ by $justification$. In other words, $justification$ should prove that property P is true in the context Φ. When justification is a simple explanation, of the form $\{explanation\}$, then we have a basic mathematical fact, which we can check directly. Otherwise, the justification has nested tasks, in which case we use the checklist for justifications to see that the justification is correct.

8. CHECKING CORRECTNESS

External context is Φ: Prove that

- • $?x : T : Q(x)$
- \- A_1

  $\vdots$

- \- A_m

- $+$ justification$_1$ $\Phi, A_1, \ldots, A_m$

  P_1 $\vdash P_1$

  $\vdots$

- $+$ justification$_n$ $\Phi, A_1, \ldots, A_m, P_1, \ldots, P_{n-1}$

  P_n $\vdash P_n$

- $+$ $y_1 : T_1$ justification$_{n+1}$ $\Phi, A_1, \ldots, A_m, P_1, \ldots, P_n$

  Q_1 $\vdash (\exists y_1 : T_1 : Q_1)$

  $\vdots$

- $+$ $y_h : T_h$ justification$_{n+h}$ $\Phi, A_1, \ldots, A_m, P_1, \ldots, P_n, Q_1, \ldots, Q_{h-1}$

  Q_h $\vdash (\exists y_h : T_h : Q_h)$

- $\Vdash$ justification$_0$ $\Phi, A_1, \ldots, A_m, P_1, \ldots, P_n, Q_1, \ldots, Q_h, t_0 \sim_1 t_1, \ldots, t_{k-1} \sim_k t_k$

  t_0 $\vdash Q(t) \wedge t \in T$

- $\sim_1$ justification$_{n+h+1}$ $\Phi, A_1, \ldots, A_m, P_1, \ldots, P_n, Q_1, \ldots, Q_h$

  t_1 $\vdash t_0 \sim_1 t_1$

  $\vdots$

- $\sim_k$ justification$_{n+h+k}$ $\Phi, A_1, \ldots, A_m, P_1, \ldots, P_n, Q_1, \ldots, Q_h$

  t_k $\vdash t_{k-1} \sim_k t_k$

- $\square$ $x = t$

Figure 8.1: Checklist for task

For an all-question $!x : T : Q(x)$, the answer is of the form $R(x)$, so *justification$_0$*

8.3. Checklists for Structured Derivations

then has to prove

$$\Phi, A_1, \ldots, A_m, P_1, \ldots, P_n, Q_1, \ldots, Q_h, t_0 \sim_1 t_1, \ldots, t_{k-1} \sim_k t_k, x \in T$$
$$\vdash R(x) \equiv Q(x)$$

Checklist for a justification The following is a checklist for a justification with nested tasks.

Prove $\Phi \vdash Q$ when *justification* has the form below:

{*explanation*}   prove that $\Phi, (\Phi \wedge \Phi_1 \Rightarrow Q_1), \ldots, (\Phi \wedge \Phi_r \Rightarrow Q_r) \vdash Q$

- Q_1 prove that task 1 is correct in context Φ
- Φ_1

⋮

□

⋮

- Q_r prove that task r is correct in context Φ
- Φ_r

⋮

□

Figure 8.2: Checklist for justification

We assume here that the nested tasks are all proof tasks. As we showed earlier, any task can be written as an equivalent proof task. The first nested task above shows that Q_1 is true in the context Φ and Φ_1, the second that Q_2 is true in the context Φ and Φ_2, ..., and the last shows that Q_r is true in the context Φ and Φ_r. All this information can then be used to support the explanation why Q is true in the context Φ.

Checklist for structured derivation in context Φ The checklist for a structured derivation has essentially the same proof steps as an observation in a task:

8. CHECKING CORRECTNESS

External context is Φ

$\vdots$

[m] P_m

$\vdots$

[n]   *justification*$_n$ prove that $\Phi, P_1, \ldots, P_{n-1} \vdash P_n$

      P_n

$\vdots$

[k] $x_k : T_k$ *justification*$_k$ prove that $\Phi, P_1, \ldots, P_{k-1} \vdash (\exists x_k : T_k : P_k)$

      P_k

$\vdots$

Figure 8.3: Checklist for derivation

CHAPTER **9**

Background on Structured Derivations

Edsger W. Dijkstra, one of the great pioneers of computer science, worked together with his colleagues Wim Feijen and Nettie van Gasteren on methods for making proofs about program correctness as easy and intuitive as possible. They developed a notation that is known as *calculational proofs* [11, 28, 12]. They wanted to carry out mathematical proofs and derivations in the same way as in traditional calculations, when solving equations, simplifying expressions or calculating values of functions. They used logical rules to calculate the truth of mathematical statements in the same way as we use algebraic rules to simplify expressions. The calculational style introduced the idea of explicit justifications on separate lines. This proof style has been adopted quite widely in articles and text books on programming methods, in particular in the context of formal (or logical, mathematical) methods for constructing correct programs. The approach is used in, e.g., the textbooks by David Gries and Fred Schneider [16], Jan van de Snepscheut [27] and Ann Kaldewej [18]. Gries and Schneider have also proposed using calculational proofs in high school teaching [15, 14, 17] and have argued for the advantages of this method in practical mathematics education.

Dijkstra's calculational proof style corresponds to what we in this book call *structured calculations*. Dijkstra's and his colleagues' work has been the main inspiration and the starting point for our own work. Joakim von Wright and I developed *structured derivations* as an extension of Dijkstra's notation for calculations. We originally presented the method in our book on *refinement calculus* [8], as well as in a journal paper [4]. We used structured derivations throughout the book, to prove a large number of theorems and lemmas of varying complexity, mainly in lattice theory and programming logic. While Dijkstra's original calculational proofs were based on a version of first-order predicate calculus and a Hilbert-style proof system, we have adopted Gentzen-style natural deduction and higher order logic as the foundations for structured derivations. This has allowed us to add nested derivations with a simple logical interpretation. Higher order logic was invented by Alonzo Church [10] in the 1940s. We based our approach on a variant of this logic by Michael Gordon and Tom Melham [13], developed for the interactive theorem prover HOL.

9. Background on Structured Derivations

The experiences that we had of using structured derivations in our book were very positive, which prompted us to look at whether structured derivations also could be used in ordinary mathematics teaching [9]. Starting in the year 2000, we have conducted a large number of pilot studies on the use of structured derivations in class teaching, focusing on high school mathematics and introductory mathematics courses in universities [5, 6, 21, 7]. The results have been very encouraging. The students see the method as different but not particularly difficult. They say that the teacher's proofs and derivations are easier to understand when they are presented as structured derivations. They also gain a better understanding of their own proofs when written in this way, and find it is easier to detect errors in their proofs. The teachers appreciate the method because it makes it is easier to check students' solutions, to see where they made mistakes and how they had misunderstood things. The biggest drawback of structured derivations usually mentioned by students is that the derivations tend to become longer. This is because each step has to be explicitly justified. We actually see this is as an important advantage, since it means that the students are carefully thinking about and justifying each step in their solution. The teachers feel that requiring explicit justifications leads to a deeper understanding of mathematics and to a better competence in applying mathematics to practical problem solving.

We continued to develop structured derivations, based on feedback from these pilot studies. A later version of structured derivations [3] added observations as new features for derivations, and showed how structured derivations could be seen as a unification of the three main proof paradigms in use today: forward derivation, backward derivation and calculation. The structured derivations method presented in this book is a further extension of the method presented in [3], adding definitions and a more precise treatment of questions and answers in tasks, as well as a more general notion of structured derivations that is better suited for mathematical modeling.

The structured derivation method has been developed in a sequence of research projects at the *Learning and Reasoning Laboratory* of *TUCS* (Abo Akademi University and University of Turku) in 2000 - 2014. The research has been funded by the Academy of Finland, the Technology Development Center of Finland (TEKES), the Technology Industry in Finland, the European Union and the Swedish Cultural Foundation in Finland. The method has been tested on a larger scale in a recent EU-project, the E-math project in 2011-13. This project piloted structured derivations in 15 high schools in Finland, Sweden and Estonia. Approximately 1 000 students participated in these pilots, which covered first year high school courses in mathematics (see http://emath.eu/ for more information about this project). We have written a series of interactive text books in e-book format for high school mathematics, all based on structured derivations. This series covers the full advanced mathematics curriculum for Finnish high schools, and is expected to be completed in 2016.

There are a not that many alternative approaches to build more precise but still human readable mathematical proofs. Leslie Lamport proposed a Gentzen-like proof style where indentation was used as a structuring device [19]. The Hilbert-like proof style for geometry has been tried in schools using a two-column proof format (see e.g., en.wikibooks.org/wiki/Geometry/Chapter_2). Interactive theorem provers like Isabelle [23] (e.g., the Isar front end [29]), Mizar [25, 26] and PVS [22] have also been equipped with more user friendly front ends for reading and writing proofs. However, these front ends usually target advanced users, and are not suitable as such for teaching mathematical proofs at the secondary education levels.

APPENDIX **A**

Syntax

We will provide a top-down definition of structured derivations, starting with the most general concepts, and showing how these are defined with more basic notions.

A.1 Derivations

We start with defining the overall syntax of structured derivations. A *derivation* is a sequence of *derivation steps*. The box below defines the syntax of structured derivations.

> *derivation*
> *derivation_step*
>
> ⋮
>
> *derivation_step*

The box should be interpreted as follows: a (structured) derivation is written as a list of successive derivation steps, written one under the other, each step starting on a new line. The three dots say that there may be zero, one or more derivation steps in this list.

Concepts that are defined later are colored blue. Concepts that are taken as primitive are marked with other colors.

A *derivation step* is either an *assumption*, an *observation* or a *task*.

> *derivation_step*
> *assumption* | *observation* | *task*

A. SYNTAX

The vertical bar "|" is used to separate the alternatives from each other. We explain below how to write assumptions, observations and tasks.

A.2 Assumptions

We have two different kinds of *assumptions*: *declarations* and *constraints*.

assumption
aid   *declaration* ',' ... ',' *declaration* | *constraint*

We mark a derivation step with an *assumption identifier* , written in the first column. The assumption identifier can be either "-", or a small letter in parenthesis (like (a), (b), (c), ...). In the second column, we write a *declaration* or a *constraint*. An assumption is a *logical proposition* (logical statement) that we may assume to be true without justification.

A *declaration* is a list of a names (for variables and constants) together with the domain of acceptable values that can be assigned to the name.

declaration
name ':' *domain*

The name is either a variable name or a constant name. The domain is some set of values, like $\mathbb{R}$ (real numbers) or $\mathbb{N}$ (natural numbers). Note that the ":" between the name and the domain is written out explicitly. The domain can, e.g., be the real numbers $\mathbb{R}$, or the natural numbers $\mathbb{N}$, or the positive natural numbers $\mathbb{N}^+$, or it can, e.g., be a function from real numbers to real numbers, $\mathbb{R} \to \mathbb{R}$.

A *constraint* is a logical *proposition* that we may assume is true in the derivation.

constraint
proposition

A.3 Observations

An *observation* is either a *fact* or a *definition*.

> **observation**
> *oid* fact | definition

We identify an *observation* with an *observation identifier* *oid* in the first column. This is either a "+" sign, or a number in square brackets, like in "[1], [2], [3], ...". The observation identifier is followed by a *fact* or a *definition*, written in the second column.

A *fact* is a *proposition* which follows from earlier assumptions and observations. We write a *fact* in the following way:

> **fact**
> *justification*
>
> *proposition*

The justification gives an argument to convinces ourselves (and others) that the fact is a consequence of the preceding steps of the derivation.

A *definition* introduces one or more new *names*, together with a *justification* that shows that these names are well-defined by the *proposition* on the next line. A definition is written as follows:

> **definition**
> *declaration* ',' ... ',' *declaration*
>
> *justification*
>
> *proposition*

A.4 Tasks

There are two kinds of *tasks*: *calculation tasks* and *general tasks*.

> **task**
> *calculation_task* | *general_task*

A. Syntax

A *general task* is as follows:

general task	
tid	*question*
⋮	
	assumption
⋮	
	observation
'⊩'	*conclusion*
	calculation
'□'	*answer*

A task starts with a *task identifier* *tid* in the first column. This can be either a bullet "•", or a capital letter like in "A., B., C.". The task ends with a square "□" in the first column. The *conclusion* following the *proof sign* "⊩" explains why the answer is correct. The vertical dots preceding *assumption* indicate that we may have zero or more assumptions, and similarly for *observation*.

The general form of a *question* is

question
('?' | '!') *declaration* ',' ... ',' *declaration* ':' *proposition*

We have two alternative forms for questions. A question mark means that we are looking for ***some*** values for the declared variables that make the logical *proposition* true, while the exclamation mark means that we are looking for ***all*** values of the declared variables that make the *proposition* true.

The *conclusion* is a *justification* that explains why the answer is correct:

| *justification* |

A.5. Calculations

The *answer* is a logical *proposition* that restricts the values of the variables included in the question:

answer
  proposition

In most cases we put additional restrictions on what kind of answers are acceptable. These restrictions are, however, very much dependent on traditions and conventions, and we will not try to capture them here.

A *calculation task* is of the the simple form

calculation task
  tid   *calculation*
  '□'

A.5 Calculations

A *calculation* is written as follows:

calculation
          expression
  rel   *justification*
          expression
  ⋮
  rel   *justification*
          expression

The three dots "⋮" show that we can add zero or more steps to the first step. Every calculation step has two lines, one with a *relation* and a *justification*, and one with an *expression*.

119

A.6 Justifications

A *justification* can be a simple *explanation*, enclosed in curly brackets, or it may be based on solving some auxiliary tasks. The auxiliary (or nested) *tasks* are written one step to the right, i.e., they start in the same column as the explanation in curly brackets. The derivation returns to the previous level after the nested tasks.

justification
'{' *explanation* '}'

⋮

task

The nested tasks thus begins in the second column of the original task, since they are indented one step. There may be zero or more nested *tasks*. The place where the original task continues may be indicated by an ellipsis ("...") in the first column.

Note that a *task* is explained in terms of *justifications*, and *justifications* are explained in terms of *tasks*. We thus have a *recursive* definition of tasks: a task contains justifications, which in turn can contain nested tasks. The nested tasks can then again contain justifications, which again can contain nested tasks, etc. We can thus have any number of tasks nested inside each other. The recursion ends when we justify a step without introducing new nested tasks.

A.7 What Has Not Been Defined

Let us finally enumerate the syntactic constructions that have **not** been defined above:

proposition	:	a logical proposition
explanation	:	an argument for why a proposition is true
expression	:	a mathematical expression
rel	:	a binary relation
name	:	a notation, constant or variable
domain	:	a value domain

The syntax for these constructs can be freely chosen, based on the specific mathematical domain on which the derivation is based on.

A.8 Abstract Syntax of Structured Derivations

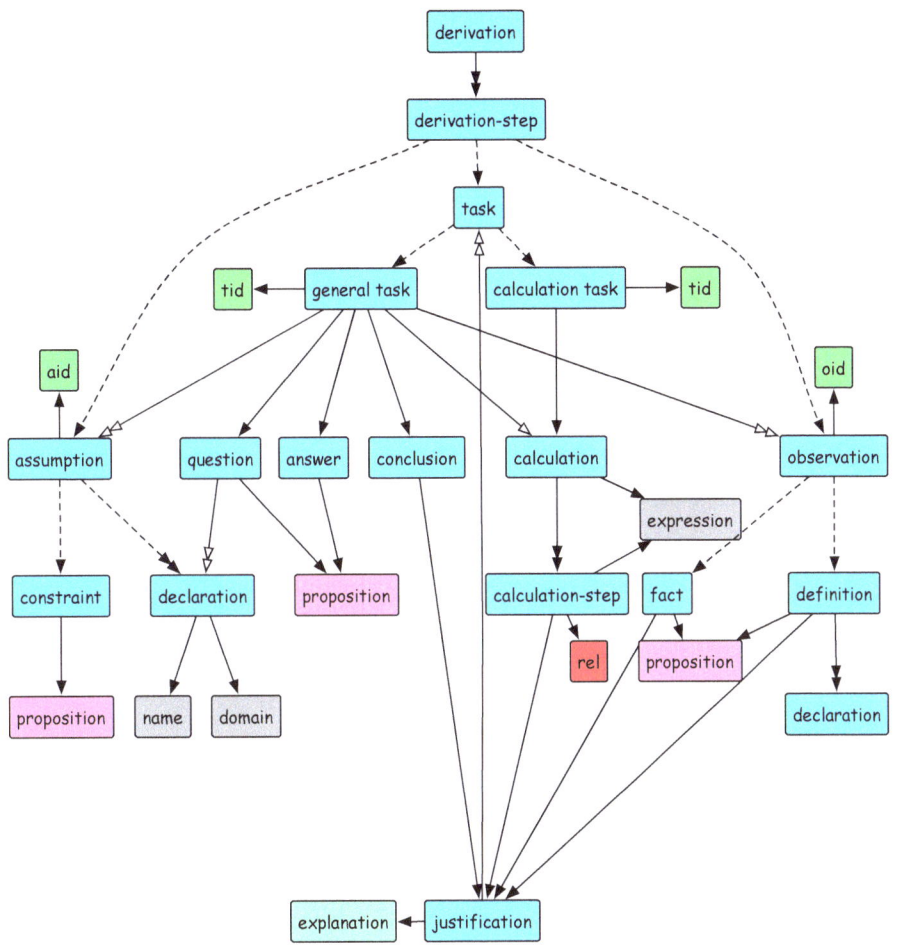

Legend:
- blue boxes aare nonterminals,
- other colors are terminals
- dashed arrows show alternatives
- solid arrows show components
- single black arrowhead shows one component is required
- single open arrowhead shows optional component
- multiple black arrowhead shows one or more components
- multiple open arrowheads show zero or more components

APPENDIX B

Answers to assignments

Chapter 2

1. a^{-1}
2. $x = 0$
3. $x = 3 \vee x = -8$ (i.e. $x = 3$ or $x = -8$)
4. $x = -\frac{1}{2} \vee x = 0 \vee x = 7$
5. 2
6. $2x \cos(2x) - 2x^2 \sin(2x)$
7. $x = 5 \wedge y = 7$ (i.e. $x = 5$ and $y = 7$)
8. Proofs need no answers
9. $x = 12 \vee x = -4$

Chapter 3

1. $x = -\frac{9}{5}$
2. $x = 1$
3. $x = \sqrt[3]{2}$
4. $x = e$
5. Yes
7. 3
9. $2^n n!$

B. Answers to assignments

Chapter 4

1. $x = 5 \land y = 17 \land z = 9$
2. $x = 3 \land y = \frac{1}{3} \land z = 6$
3. $x = \frac{13}{5}$
4. $x < -8 \lor x > -2$
5. $x = -3 \lor x = 5$
6. Yes
7. It intersects the xy-plane in the point (5.2, 3.8, 0)
8. The number is 13

Chapter 5

3. $2 < x \leq \sqrt{10}$
5. (4, 0, 1)

Chapter 6

1. 2.5 pizzas
2. It is $\frac{1}{10}$
3. Anna mixed the juice at a ratio of 3 : 11
4. The person could be on their death bed arranging cards and they would still have barely started the task (the age of the universe would also be woefully insufficient as would the squared and cubed ages of the universe)
5. The ratio of the mixtures should be 3 parts of the stronger and 4 parts of the weaker sauce
6. The increase in price did not pay off!
7. Approximately $2.5 \cdot 10^{22}$ joules of energy was released

Chapter 7

1. $x = 0 \lor x = 1$, when n is even, $x = -1 \lor x = 0 \lor x = 1$, when n is odd
2. $x < -1 \lor -1 < x < 0 \lor x > 1$
3. a) Approximately $1600\,\text{km}$ b) The volume of Cube-Sedna is approximately $1.5 \cdot 10^9 \text{km}^3$. This is approximately 63% of the original volume
4. a) $102\,\text{dm}^3$ b) Approximately $91\,\text{dm}^3$ of gunpowder

5. a) $\frac{2}{11}$, b) $\frac{10}{33}$, c) $\frac{4}{165}$.

6. a) $4x^3 + 5$ b) 37 c) $f(x) = \left(\frac{5}{4}\right)^{\frac{4}{3}} - 5 \cdot \sqrt[3]{\frac{5}{4}} + 2 \approx -2.03956\ldots$ at $x = -\sqrt[3]{\frac{5}{4}}$

7. a) 12 000 volume units, b) $1.54\,\text{m}^3$ c) $1\,080\,\text{kg}$ of wood d) 2.76 liters of varnish

Bibliography

[1] Ralph-Johan Back. *Correctness Preserving Program Refinements: Proof Theory and Applications*, volume 131 of *Mathematical Center Tracts*. Mathematical Centre, Amsterdam, The Netherlands, 1980.

[2] Ralph-Johan Back. A calculus of refinements for program derivations. *Acta Informatica*, 25:593–624, 1988.

[3] Ralph-Johan Back. Structured Derivations: a Unified Proof Style for Teaching Mathematics. *Formal Aspects of Computing*, 22(5):629–661, 2010.

[4] Ralph-Johan Back, Jim Grundy, and Joakim von Wright. Structured calculational proof. *Formal Aspects of Computing*, 9:469–483, 1998.

[5] Ralph-Johan Back, Linda Mannila, Mia Peltomaki, and Patrick Sibelius. Structured derivations: A logic based approach to teaching mathematics. In *FORMED 2008: Formal Methods in Computer Science Education, Budapest*, 2008.

[6] Ralph-Johan Back, Linda Mannila, and Solveig Wallin. Student justifications in high school mathematics. In *CERME 6*, January 2009.

[7] Ralph-Johan Back, Linda Mannila, and Solveig Wallin. "It Takes Me Longer, but I Understand Better" - Student Feedback on Structured Derivations. In *International Journal of Mathematical Education in Science and Technology*, volume 41, pages 575–593, 2010.

[8] Ralph-Johan Back and Joakim von Wright. *Refinement Calculus: A Systematic Introduction*. Springer-Verlag, 1998. Graduate Texts in Computer Science.

[9] Ralph-Johan Back and Joakim von Wright. A method for teaching rigorous mathematical reasoning. In *Proceedings of Int. Conference on Technology of Mathematics*, University of Plymouth, UK, Aug 1999.

[10] A. Church. A formulation of the simple theory of types. *Journal of Symbolic Logic*, 5:56–68, 1940.

[11] Edsger W. Dijkstra and C. S. Scholten. *Predicate Calculus and Program Semantics*. Springer-Verlag, 1990.

[12] E.W. Dijkstra. The notational conventions I adopted, and why. *Formal Aspects of Computing*, 14:99 – 107, 2002.

[13] M.J.C. Gordon and T.F. Melham. *Introduction to HOL*. Cambridge University Press, New York, 1993.

[14] David Gries. Teaching calculation and discrimination: A more effective curriculum. *Communications of the ACM*, (34):45 – 54, 1991.

[15] David Gries. *Teaching and Learning Formal Methods*, chapter Improving the curriculum through the teaching of calculatio and discrimination, pages 181–196. Academic Press, London, 1996.

[16] David Gries and Fred Schneider. *A Logical Introduction to Discrete Mathematics*. Springer-Verlag, 1993.

[17] David Gries and Fred Schneider. Teaching math more effectively through calculational proofs. *Am. Math. Monthly*, pages 691–697, October 1995.

[18] Anne Kaldewaij. *Programming: The Derivation Of Algorithms*. Prentice Hall, 1990.

[19] Leslie Lamport. How to write a proof. *American Math. Monthly*, 102(7):600–608, 1995.

[20] Linda Mannila and Solveig Wallin. Promoting students justification skills using structured derivations. In *ICMI 19 studies*, 2009.

[21] Linda Mannila and Solveig Wallin. Promoting Students' Justification Skills Using Structured Derivations. In *Proceedings of the ICMI Study 19 Conference: Proof and Proving in Mathematics Education*, pages 64–69, Taipei, Taiwan, 2009. National Taiwan Normal University.

[22] Sam Owre, Natarajan Shankar, and John Rushby. PVS: A prototype verification system. In *CADE 11*, Saratoga Springs, NY, June 1992.

[23] L. C. Paulson. Isabelle: the next 700 theorem provers. In P. Odifreddi, editor, *Logic and Computer Science*, pages 361–386. Academic Press, 1990.

[24] Mia Peltomäki and Ralph-Johan Back. An empirical evaluation of structured derivations in high school mathematics. In *ICMI-19 studies*, Taipei, Taiwan, 2009.

[25] A. Trybulec. The Mizar logic information language. In *Studies in Logic, Grammar and Rhetoric*, volume 1. Bialystok, 1980.

[26] A. Trybulec and P. Rudnicki. On equivalents of well-foundedness: An experiment in Mizar. *Journal of Automated Reasoning*, 23:197–234, 1999.

[27] Jan L. A. van de Snepscheut. *What computing is all about*. Springer Verlag, 1993.

[28] A. J. M. van Gasteren. *On the Shape of Mathematical Arguments*. Lecture Notes in Computer Science. Springer-Verlag, Berlin, 1990.

[29] Markus Wenzel. Isar - a generic interpretative approach to readable formal proof documents. In Y. Bertot, G. Dowek, A. Hirschowitz, C. Paulin, and L. Thery, editors, *Theorem Proving in Higher Order Logics, 12th International Conference, TPHOLs'99*, volume 1690 of *LNCS*. Springer Verlag, 1999.

www.ingramcontent.com/pod-product-compliance
Lightning Source LLC
Chambersburg PA
CBHW041511220426
43661CB00047B/1530